DATE DUE

GAYLORD			PRINTED IN U.S.A.

THE SILVER FOXES ARE DEAD

and other plays

THE
SILVER
FOXES
ARE
DEAD
and other plays
by Jakov Lind

translated by Ralph Manheim

HILL & WANG
New York

Published in the United States of America by Hill & Wang, Inc.

STANDARD BOOK NUMBER (clothbound edition): 8090–8674–3
STANDARD BOOK NUMBER (paperback edition): 8090–0744–4

Library of Congress catalog card number: 69–16826
First American edition March 1969

The plays were originally broadcast as follows:
Anna Laub by Suddeutscher Rundfunk, Stuttgart, 1964
Das Sterben der Silberfüchse by Norddeutscher Rundfunk, Hamburg, 1965
Hunger by Hessischer Rundfunk, Frankfurt-am-Main, 1966
Angst by Bayrischer Rundfunk, Munich, 1967

All inquiries concerning the rights for professional or amateur stock production should be directed to Joan Daves, 145 East 49th Street, New York, N.Y. 10017

Manufactured in the United States of America

1234567890

CONTENTS

The Silver Foxes Are Dead

CHARACTERS

JEREMIAH PETZEL, aged thirty-five and later
VERA, aged twenty-four and later
ROBERT, same age as Petzel
DR FRIEDRICH, about forty
FRANZ, an apprentice, about thirty

Places

A large pet shop
Jeremiah Petzel's apartment
A cellar workshop
The countryside
A barn
A room in a private hospital
A hotel room

Time

1945, 1946, 1960, the present.

SCENE ONE (1945)

*In the country. The twittering of birds blends into the song
of a single bird. The bleating of a goat. Wind in the trees.*

JEREMIAH PETZEL *is lying on the grass, humming a tune.*

ROBERT. Halt, or I fire. Hands up.

> ROBERT *takes a few steps through the grass.*

What's that on your arm?

PETZEL. A number.

ROBERT. And this here? A yellow patch. What's it for?

PETZEL. The Star of Bethlehem. Only Jews are allowed to
wear it.

ROBERT. Only Jews. That's fine. Let's go.

PETZEL (*gasping for air*). No, you're not taking me to a camp ...
(*He runs away.*) No, no.

ROBERT (*runs after him, panting*). Halt. Don't move. (*Panting.*)
Halt. I want that jacket. I like the stripes. I've always wanted
a jacket like that. With a decoration. Give it here. It fits
perfectly ... Here's mine.

PETZEL. It's too big. I've lost weight.

ROBERT. Just tighten the belt. You'll grow into it ... You can
make anything fit if you have to.

PETZEL. I'm not going to a camp. Go ahead and shoot.
I'm not going ...

ROBERT. Who said anything about a camp? We're not going
to any camp, but we're not staying here either ... Get
going ... We can't let them find us here ... I'll lead the
way ... (*An object falls in the grass.*) What good is an empty
revolver? There ... now follow me ... I know the terrain.
(*He whistles a march, they walk a while.*) What's your name
anyway?

PETZEL. Jeremiah Petzel.

ROBERT. Well, Jeremiah, I've got news for you ... (*He whistles.*) The war's over.

PETZEL. What? What's over?

ROBERT. The war ... I'd almost forgotten.

PETZEL. What? What about the war?

ROBERT. We've capitulated.

PETZEL. Who says so?

ROBERT. At eleven o'clock this morning.

PETZEL (*slow to understand*). The war's been over ... since eleven o'clock ... how come I'm still here?

ROBERT. My name's Robert. Yes, you're still here. We're both here. Alive and kicking. Both of us. It's a warm afternoon in May.

ROBERT and PETZEL (*laugh wildly and hysterically, alternately, then together, only stopping occasionally to say*). It's a warm afternoon in May.

SCENE TWO (*1945*)

Tanks, trucks and American soldiers' songs slowly fading in and out. A hayloft.

ROBERT. Money for blood. Paper for liquid. Well, what do you say? Jeremiah, say something for God's sake.

PETZEL (*after a brief pause*). Robert, I can't do it.

ROBERT (*impatiently*). You can't do it. You can't do it. Why not? If they test me, I'm done for. You've got nothing to be afraid of. You've got your number.

PETZEL. You're out of your mind.

ROBERT. Fifty thousand cash for the first twenty years. And then we'll see. My last offer.

PETZEL. How many did you shoot?

ROBERT. I was a common clerk.

PETZEL. And torture?

ROBERT. I only worked in an office.

PETZEL (*jumps up, seizes* ROBERT *in a fury and shakes him*).
All right, what did you do? What crimes did you commit,
you swine? Speak up or I'll throw you out of the window.
The Americans will pick you up.

ROBERT. Do what you please, I've told you the truth. I was
a simple clerk at the property custodian's office. I never
hurt anybody. But I'm a German. Don't you see? The
Germans robbed and murdered all over Europe. For five
years. Right? Right. Nobody knows if I had anything to
do with it or not. I can talk myself blue in the face, who's
going to make them believe me? (*He shouts excitedly.*) But
if they give me a blood test and find Jewish blood, there's
my alibi. Fifty thousand dollars.

PETZEL. Jewish blood?

ROBERT. You're a Jew, aren't you?

PETZEL. Yes.

ROBERT. Then you've got Jewish blood.

PETZEL. Yes, of course.

ROBERT. Give me your blood, I'll give you mine and money
as well. We both stand to gain.

PETZEL. I come of a very good family.

ROBERT. Glad to hear it.

PETZEL. Sixteen Jewish grandparents.

ROBERT. Better and better.

PETZEL. A family of rabbis. The wonder-working rabbi of
Kishenev is a relative.

ROBERT. A wonder-working rabbi? Perfect!

PETZEL. I can't do it.

ROBERT. Don't be sentimental. Don't be a blockhead. What
good did your Jewish blood ever do you? (*He sees* JEREMIAH
growing thoughtful.) Misery, that's what it brought you.

PETZEL. It didn't bring me happiness, it almost cost me my

life. (*After brief reflection.*) Fifty thousand for twenty years.
I agree. It's absurd, it's madness. But if we both stand to
gain by it, call it a deal.

ROBERT (*holds out his hand*). Twenty years.

    PETZEL *shakes it.*

SCENE THREE (*1945*)

DR FRIEDRICH. One hour more, gentlemen, and the whole
thing will be over. (*To* PETZEL.) It makes a difference,
doesn't it, a little German blood in your veins. How do
you feel?

PETZEL (*weary and faint*). Fine. I feel bad already.

DR FRIEDRICH (*smiles at Robert*). And you, my boy? Feeling
Jewish?

ROBERT (*smiles contentedly*). Does it hurt! Does it hurt!

DR FRIEDRICH. You'll get used to it. But otherwise you're
satisfied? Do you want something to eat?

ROBERT. Do I want something to eat!

    The nurse feeds the patients alternately.

PETZEL. He's starting to talk like me. You don't say: Do I
want to eat! You say: Yes, please. And you don't say: does
it hurt! You say: I'm feeling fine, thank you.

DR FRIEDRICH (*rubbing his hands*). Only an hour, gentlemen,
and our operation will be completed. And in the nick of
time, Mr Robert. They're already started denazifying.
Investigating people inside and out. And you can sit back
and laugh. When you think of all the things we've done!
Did you see that film yesterday? I'm telling you, those
concentration camps were no credit to us. Such things are
hard to forgive. But you're a lucky man. You've taken your
precautions before it's too late. How did you ever find him?

ROBERT. By accident. In the woods.

DR FRIEDRICH. You can consider yourself very fortunate. You don't see many people in the woods at this time of year, certainly not Jews – not in the last twelve years.

PETZEL (*in pain*). Not surprising. The Jews have no love of nature. They're stay-at-homes. All Jews are pale.

DR FRIEDRICH (*beaming*). It's taking effect, it's taking effect. The new blood has reached the brain cells.

PETZEL. Take it from me, doctor, the Jews didn't deserve any better than they got. They should have shown more courage.

DR FRIEDRICH. He's already speaking like one of us. (*Critically.*) But don't overdo it. Let's not get anti-Semitic. Prejudices are human, lenience is in order. But watch your step with anti-Semitism, especially in the next few weeks. Take it easy for a while. (*He takes a bill from his wallet and holds it in front of* ROBERT'*s face.*) I've made up your bill. Are you paying in jewellery or in dollars?

ROBERT (*wearily*). Dollars.

SCENE FOUR (*1946*)

PETZEL. Ten, twenty, two hundred ... It's dwindling fast, and the first year is hardly over.

VERA. You sent for me?

PETZEL. Yes. Please take a letter. We have the honour to inform you that the firm of Jeremiah Petzel and Co. is opening a pet shop on Thursday, 16th May, 1946, at 27 Underberg Street. We specialize in tropical varieties. But you will also find the largest selection of native songbirds in the American occupation zone.

VERA. How long are you going to go on living at the hotel?

PETZEL. I like hotels. In hotels you only meet strangers. I'm a stranger myself. Everything in this country is strange to me. I hardly understand what the people say. At home, in the old days, long ago, I understood every word. But it's so long ago I've forgotten everything. It gets worse every day. A stranger understands nothing.

VERA. Are you a Jew or are you not a Jew, Jeremiah?

PETZEL. I don't remember.

VERA. What do you mean, you don't remember?

PETZEL. I used to know; now I've forgotten that as well. On the one hand yes, on the other hand no, in my mind yes, in my feet no. And sometimes it's the other way round.

VERA. But you can't help knowing a thing like that. Have you Jewish blood or haven't you?

PETZEL. Jewish blood? Certainly not.

VERA. Then you're not a Jew.

PETZEL. Then I'm not a Jew. (*He ponders.*) What's Jewish blood or non-Jewish blood anyway? What nonsense is that? How can blood be Jewish or non-Jewish? Blood is blood. But then, again, maybe not. Everybody believes in blood. But what do they mean?

VERA. If we didn't know the difference, we couldn't tell people apart.

PETZEL. Right. You've got to be able to tell people apart. Now I see.

VERA. It's not that any race is better or worse. There is no reason for people to hate each other because of it, but there has to be a difference.

PETZEL. Yes, of course, there has to be a difference. Or we couldn't tell people apart. Rich and poor, sick and healthy, clever and stupid aren't enough. We need blood.

SCENE FIVE (1960)

A hotel room.

JEREMIAH PETZEL *and* VERA. *A knock at the door.*

PETZEL. Come in.

ROBERT. Jeremiah Petzel? Do you remember me? Do you know who I am?

PETZEL. Vera, take the mail to the post office and then take yourself to the pictures.

VERA. I don't like the pictures, I don't want to go to the pictures. Every night for ten years I've had to go to the pictures.

PETZEL. Not every night. That's an exaggeration. But tonight I have a guest I've been expecting for fifteen years. This is 1960. Yes, exactly fifteen years.

VERA *leaves the room slamming the door behind her.*

ROBERT. Bad news.

PETZEL. I can see that. You're in rags.

ROBERT. That's nothing. There's something worse. I've got cancer. Two years to go at the very most.

PETZEL. Our contract says five.

ROBERT. Only two to live. Bad blood condition.

PETZEL. What do the doctors say?

ROBERT. They've given me up. I'm finished.

PETZEL. Do you want money?

ROBERT. You cheated me.

PETZEL. I cheated you?

ROBERT. The Americans didn't make any blood tests.

PETZEL. No blood tests? You amaze me.

ROBERT. No blood tests. The whole business with the blood was a swindle. Give me a blood test, I said. Go ahead. But they only questioned me. I told them the truth, that I was

in the Party, only a rank-and-file member, never held any
office. Just like everybody else. And that my work at the
property custodian's was only a job.

PETZEL. What did they say?

ROBERT. They hardly listened. I said to them: Gentlemen,
I'm sorry.

PETZEL. That's all?

ROBERT. That's all. I said: I honestly and sincerely regret
everything. They looked out the window and ... sent me
home.

PETZEL. Well, there you are. (*To himself*.) He's sorry, and
nobody's interested. He repents and nobody comforts him.

ROBERT. I could kill myself.

PETZEL. What's the use? If the doctors only give you two
years.

ROBERT. You wish I were dead, don't you?

PETZEL. And how! But I won't do anything about it. I have
the good blood now and you the bad. That's enough.

ROBERT (*furious*). You knew. You knew it all the time.

PETZEL. No, on my word of honour, I didn't. My health has
always been good. Except in the concentration camp, where
I nearly died. Sheer luck if I didn't. But it was my bad blood
that sent me there, you're right about that. I'm not sure
if it was really that bad. All I know is it almost did me in.

SCENE SIX (*1960*)

*Later the same evening. The two of them are sitting by the
window in the dusk, looking out at the street; they are drinking.*

PETZEL. Do you think both of us were crazy, or only you?

ROBERT. Only me. I believed in it. I believed in Jewish blood
and Aryan blood, and so help me God, I still do.

PETZEL. You still do, Robert? You still do? Oh well, I understand . . . You must think about blood a good deal.

ROBERT. Let's have another drink. (*He pours himself a drink.*) I don't want to think about anything. This can't go on.

PETZEL. Look here, I'm not going through with another transfusion, and certainly not now. You have no grounds for complaint. I won't listen. I understand you, I sympathize. But more than that I can't do. You attacked me in the woods.

ROBERT. That's a long time ago.

PETZEL. Long or short. Real madness has lasting consequences. There's a kind of real madness that's so insidious you can't help wondering if there's enough reason in the world to understand what real madness is. They say atomic fall-out affects the human brain. What do you think?

ROBERT. There wasn't any atomic fall-out before the war.

PETZEL. Then there was something else. How come I was in a concentration camp and you weren't?

ROBERT. Ask the Nazis.

PETZEL. But *you* were a Nazi.

ROBERT. Yes, but not a real one, you know that. I was only a simple party member. Like everybody else.

PETZEL. Tell me this. Were there any real Nazis in Germany?

ROBERT. Of course. In the SS. Who guarded you in the camp? The SS, wasn't it?

PETZEL. Yes, but would I have been sent there if all the people in the street had resisted?

ROBERT. Don't talk nonsense. Why should all the people in the street resist when a Jew is being arrested?

PETZEL. Why not?

ROBERT. Why should they? Anyway, by the time the war broke out it was too late. Right after '33 it was too late.

PETZEL. And earlier?

ROBERT. Earlier it was too late, too. People don't like Jews, it's always been like that.

PETZEL. Why don't they like Jews?

ROBERT. I don't know. Maybe because they're weak. Because they're unhealthy.

PETZEL. What do you mean? Do you think all Jews have cancer?

ROBERT. Anyway, they let themselves be killed as if they had some terrible disease.

PETZEL. I've opened a pet shop. We have exotic animals and lots of birds. Native songbirds. The largest collection in the Federal Republic. You could take care of my birds, for instance. Can you clean out cages? Can you feed animals?

ROBERT. What's the pay?

PETZEL. The going wage for that kind of work. You won't get rich.

ROBERT. Is there still any left?

PETZEL. Any what?

ROBERT. Any of my money?

PETZEL. Less and less. I've invested it in silver foxes. Silver foxes are the thing nowadays. Only you've got to know your silver foxes.

ROBERT. Give it back. I'd know what to do with it.

PETZEL. What? Now all of a sudden? Buy Chinese blood?

ROBERT. Why Chinese blood?

PETZEL. A little coloured blood will come in handy one of these days.

ROBERT (*slightly drunk, raises the bottle to hit* PETZEL *over the head*). Give me my money!

PETZEL. No, Robert, I don't owe you a thing. Not yet. Some day perhaps. Who knows what's going to happen . . .

    VERA *appears in the room.*

VERA. I've seen four pictures. I can't stand any more.

PETZEL. Take a rest. There's another show at midnight.

SCENE SEVEN (TODAY)

A large pet shop.

> *Animals in crowded cages.* JEREMIAH PETZEL *inspects the rows of animals.* FRANZ, *his helper, follows him.*

PETZEL. A few screams, a few of them still scurrying about, one's singing, this one's still nibbling, this one's eyes are glazed . . . they're going fast. You won't make it, Franz . . . it's almost over . . . put the bowl closer so he can drink. Go on, drink, drink . . . No, he can't. Another half-hour, Franz, that's all, then you can clean out the cage.

FRANZ. Half an hour? It won't last ten minutes. The sooner the better. Water won't help him, and he won't touch his meat.

PETZEL. Can't you read? What does this sign say?

FRANZ (*reading slowly*). 'Shop closing. All animals for sale at bargain prices.'

PETZEL. So you can read. Put the sign in the window. It's all over. The money's gone, dust unto dust.

FRANZ. The foxes, Mr Petzel, the foxes. They were expensive. It didn't take long.

PETZEL. Put the sign in the window, and make it quick. No one's going to buy dead animals.

SCENE EIGHT (TODAY)

An apartment.

> *Noise rises from the pet shop below.* JEREMIAH PETZEL *paces the floor restlessly. Music. The music stops suddenly.* JEREMIAH PETZEL *closes a door, the animal sounds fall silent.*

VERA. What do you mean we're closing?

PETZEL. Closing is closing. We're shutting up shop.

VERA. Yesterday you were still saying 'we're doing fine' and today we're selling out.

PETZEL. We've managed for too long. For twenty years we did fine. This can't go on. We're leaving town.

VERA (*menacingly*). We're staying right here.

PETZEL. Maybe we'll stay, but not for long. In three weeks it will all be over.

VERA. What's the matter, Jeremiah? What's wrong with you?

PETZEL. Nothing's wrong with me. We're bankrupt, that's all.

VERA. What?

PETZEL. None of this belongs to me, don't look at me like that, it never belonged to me, it's all borrowed. It's only a loan. (*Pause.*) Not even, not even . . . nothing belongs to me.

VERA. Not even what?

PETZEL. Nothing, not even my blood. Everything . . . it all belongs to him.

VERA. To him? To whom?

PETZEL. That's right, to him. To our Robert down there in the cellar, our friend Robert, our dear Robert, down in the cellar building bird cages. It all belongs to him.

VERA. And you're going to return it?

PETZEL. No. It can't go back. But it can't go on either. It can only go down . . . we'll tell him everything, everything. It's time to tell the truth, the truth is overdue. And you'll be my witness.

SCENE NINE (TODAY)

Steps are heard on the stairs.

VERA. What are you going to tell him?

PETZEL. How many ways are there of telling the truth?
 Steps.
VERA. How will he take it?
PETZEL. How *can* he take it?
 Steps.
VERA. How will he bear the truth?
PETZEL. Can anyone bear the truth?
VERA. The question is how.

SCENE TEN (TODAY)

A room full of the twittering of birds. PETZEL *and* VERA *enter.*
After a brief pause . . .

PETZEL. How's it going?
ROBERT. Badly.
PETZEL. Then you're still alive?
ROBERT (*whistles a tune*). Yes, I'm still . . . alive.
PETZEL. All this talk about the economic miracle. And look
 at you.
ROBERT. And you?
PETZEL. Giving away the merchandise. We're closing. Selling
 out. I've put a sign in the window.
ROBERT. And then what?
PETZEL. Then nothing.
ROBERT. And what's going to become of me?
PETZEL. What's going to become of you?
ROBERT. I'll croak . . . it won't be long.
PETZEL. You've got plenty of time.
ROBERT. How much time?
 PETZEL *is silent.*
  Not forever.

PETZEL. Business is business. And forever is too long anyway. For you too.

ROBERT. Robbery, you mean. Not business.

PETZEL. We have a contract . . .

ROBERT. Yes, covering twenty years. But your damn blood is rotting . . . it's killing me.

PETZEL. Killing you. That's right. Rotting. Yes. Who asked you to take it?

ROBERT. Vera, didn't you know? Naturally, he didn't tell you. Here, I'm going to take this knife . . .

VERA. What are you doing?

ROBERT. This blood that's dripping from my finger . . . this blood . . . it's his . . . and it's no good. There's cancer in it.

PETZEL. Is that my fault?

ROBERT. What do I care whose fault it is. I'm dying, Petzel, I'm dying.

PETZEL. Who asked for this deal? Me, I suppose?

ROBERT. No, I did. But now that I'm dying . . .

PETZEL. Everybody dies. You're not the only one. But now it's your turn. You don't ask why. All of a sudden you've forgotten everything . . . But forgetting won't do it. You've got to remember, Robert, not forget. This was bound to happen. It had to turn out exactly like this. Our blood deal. Your fear of the Americans and my fear of life. And now it's caught up with us.

SCENE ELEVEN (TODAY)

ROBERT (*pauses a moment in his work*). At least I'd like to know what's become of my money.

PETZEL. I've told you, it's all gone. There was a curse on that money. Yesterday the alligator died, the day before yesterday I had to take the monkeys to the hospital to be put to sleep, and the Indian owls won't live till morning. But we'll still be able to unload the songbirds. Everything else was a miscalculation, a big mistake.

ROBERT. Why did you invest my money in animals? Why?

PETZEL. A man has to live. Concentrate on the songbirds, they'll keep us a while. Maybe.

ROBERT (*in despair*). And the silver foxes? They cost a fortune. Don't tell me they're gone too.

PETZEL (*after a short pause, solemnly*). I regret to say that the silver foxes are dead.

ROBERT (*excitedly*). That's not true. It's not possible. They were in perfect health the day before yesterday. What have you done to them?

PETZEL. Poisoned.

ROBERT. Who poisoned them?

PETZEL. I did. I poisoned them.

ROBERT (*puzzled*). You poisoned the silver foxes? Are you crazy? (*More calmly.*) Did they hit you in the concentration camp?

PETZEL. Yes, but not very much.

ROBERT. What did they do to you?

PETZEL. Sent my children to the gas chamber.

ROBERT. Is that why?

PETZEL. Who cares why? (*Screaming.*) I can't stand silver foxes, do you hear. I can't stand animals anyway. I hate them! (*On his way out.*) There's no demand for silver foxes.

ROBERT. Buying silver foxes and then killing them. You're not normal, you ought to be locked up.

PETZEL. Locked up? I've filed a petition of bankruptcy. Isn't that enough?

ROBERT. No it's not enough, not for me. You can go on living after your bankruptcy. You'll have everything you need. You'll go on living with my money, with my blood.

PETZEL (*calls back*). What do you care, if I can afford it?

ROBERT (*running out the door after him*). That thing we did was insane. It can't be true. It's unthinkable. Give me back my blood or my money or something. Do something for me, please, please, do something. Don't let me die. Forgive me my madness. I'm normal again now, perfectly normal . . . perfectly normal . . .

SCENE TWELVE (TODAY)

PETZEL. Now the poor bastard is perfectly normal . . . now . . . now that he's got one foot in the grave. It's twenty years later and still people are dying of it. People, animals. That was no ordinary war.

VERA. Here they lie: guinea-pigs from West Africa, white rats from East Africa, the three turtles, the parrot, the two Abyssinian rabbits, the baboon, the Siamese . . . The fish are floating on their backs . . .

VERA's *enumeration is interrupted by her steps and* PETZEL's, *and the cries and death-rattles of the dying animals.*

It happened so fast. It can't go on. Died one after another right here in the house . . . And I didn't know . . . nobody told me anything . . . I was at the pictures . . . always out, always at the pictures . . . I didn't know about anything.

PETZEL. No, nobody told you anything. You didn't know, that's true. But do you know any more now? And even if you'd seen everything like me, would you know any more then? Knowledge is no help to us, Vera.

VERA. But what can help us if knowledge can't? How can we save Robert? How can we help him? And what's to become of us if you destroy everything that you've built up over the years? What's to become of us all, Jeremiah? Tell me.

The whimpering of the dying animals grows louder. ROBERT's *voice joins in, shouting: 'Help me! Help me!' His shouts die down, then suddenly become very loud again.*

PETZEL (*soothingly*). Hush, Robert. Let me think. I've got to think. We've got to do something, we've got to do something ... (*He keeps repeating until the final fade-out*): something has got to be done, something has got to be done ...

Anna Laub

CHARACTERS

ANNA LAUB
KELLY
VOSS
HENRY
KARL
INA

Music, sounds, echoes. Rolling thunder in the distance, echoes of thunder; the monotonous sound of a train crossing a bridge, interspersed with regular and irregular trumpet blasts. Suddenly ANNA *is heard singing to a tune from Mahler's* Kindertotenlieder. *The whole song can be repeated in recitative.*

ANNA (*sings*).
    And wait until they fall from the sky
    striking like hammers on tin
    striking like drops on burning stones
    people in the river in flames
    the tightrope walkers fall into my net
    No one will ever escape.
    (*Speaks*). No one will ever escape.
VOSS. Anna.
ANNA (*almost defiantly*). No one will ever escape.
VOSS. Anna.
ANNA (*off-hand*). What do you want?
VOSS. Anna. How big is the biggest fish?
ANNA. As big as your big mouth.
    After each of ANNA's *answers a pause.*
VOSS. Are there streets in heaven?
ANNA. There are only fields in heaven.
INA (*thoughtfully*). Which path do I take at the crossroads?
ANNA. The one on the right.
INA. Where does the right-hand path lead?
ANNA. To the end.
HENRY. And the left-hand path?
ANNA. To the beginning.
KARL. Anna! Anna!
ANNA. Yes, Karl.
KARL. How deep is the river?

ANNA. Too shallow for you.

VOSS. Anna! Anna!

ANNA. Will you be still! It's time to sleep.

> *Heavy muffled music; at the same time sharp, clear drop.*
> *on the tin hut.*

VOSS. I'm cold. My head is bare.

ANNA. Put your cap on.

INA. We're afraid in the rain.

ANNA (*resolute*). It's late, do you hear me, it's late.

HENRY. My feet ache with the cold.

ANNA. Stretch them out.

HENRY. I want to come in with you.

ANNA. Don't you dare. This is my hut. No one comes in
with me.

INA. It's warm in there.

ANNA. Stay where you are.

KARL. It's wet out here.

ANNA. That's enough now. Go and sleep in your ditch. Or
go home.

INA. We can't go home. We want to come in with you.

ANNA. No one comes in with me. I sleep here and you stay
out there. And now be quiet.

VOSS. I'm cold.

ANNA. Go to hell. There's no room in here.

KARL (*in a quavering voice*). You fished us out of the water.

ANNA That's my business.

KARL. Now you've got to warm us.

INA. She's got to warm us.

VOSS. We want to go in by the fire.

> ANNA *opens the door – outside wind and storm. The*
> *coughing, panting, groaning and whimpering of the four*
> *wet figures in the ditch. Music.*

ANNA. Not another word. I won't listen. I saved your lives
Now I regret it.

HENRY. The rain is getting worse.

VOSS. A wet muzzle on my cheek. Who's there? Go away.

ANNA. You're dreaming. You're crazy. It's the rain.

VOSS. The rain? How can I sleep in the rain?

ANNA. You've got a mother. Go home.

ANA. Come closer, Voss, my fingers are like ice.

VOSS. I want to go in to Anna.

ANNA. I'm not a doss-house. I'm going to sleep now.

She slams the door.

For twenty-five years I've been living in this tin hut. I've fished six hundred people out of the river. Now they are lying in the fields – whimpering with cold. Rain won't wash them away. The heat won't dry them up. They cling to the ditch like the lice in my stockings. The night is a cave.

Music. ANNA *puts wood in the fire, the fire flares up, the wood crackles.*

Wet mud. Three hundred million scratch the crust. A wound that will never heal. I've got my fire. They lie outside in the ditch, not ten steps away. While this door stays shut, nobody knows if I still exist. My face is closed, my mouth is barred. My pain is no one else's. *They* fall in the water, *they* have a right to scream. *They* sink, *they* have a right to gurgle. But when I scream – I, Anna Laub, who rescued them – nobody cares. Those who don't die must keep quiet. (*She screams a long drawn-out 'Ah!'*) Quiet. Nothing. Nothing. (*She repeats her scream.*) Nothing. Dead.

She opens the door. Stylized music mingling the sounds on the bridge: pedestrians, cars, horse-drawn carts.

There they go, they don't even know I'm here. (*She screams.*) Aaaah! . . . Aah! . . . they don't want to hear me. Hey!

Hey! (*Echo.*)

VOSS (*half-asleep*). May I come in?

ANNA. Shut your trap. (*She shouts.*) Hey! hey!

KARL (*in a hoarse voice*). We're alone too.

ANNA. Quiet. Go on sleeping.

A VOICE. Yoo-hoo.

ANNA. Come on down.

VOICE. Yoo-hoo.

ANNA (*closes the door: laughs*). He won't come. He knows
A tin hut isn't a brothel. That's how it goes. The good ones
stay up top. The scum fall in the water. Anna – fishes them
out. Pumps out their lungs, dries them and feeds them –
warms them by the fire and throws them out. What falls
from the bridge belongs to me. What falls from the bridge
is useless. That's how it's always been. On May the thirtieth
when I was sick, the windows were painted with tar
Nobody went out. They crawled under my door, climbed
up and down the walls, up and down ... forced their way
up through the cracks in the floorboards. They lay in my
dishes, my clothes, in the leaves of my begonias. The ant
smelled sweet wood. They came by the millions and ate
Everything. May the thirtieth. That day the world wa
empty and dark. An eclipse? Who knows? That night
slept with skinless people. Displayed in bundles. Cu
according to weight. Christmas geese. Yet they were people
The heads were missing, but not a drop of blood on them
Made of synthetic fibre? White flesh. Without price tags
Cut. Skinned. Dreams like that don't last. Next day every
thing was the same as before. The windows were trans
parent, the ants had disappeared.

White, high walls. Only walls and windows and on th
pavements bright-coloured wool flowing by. No one mad
music. Leather beat against stone. The same as now u
there on the bridge. The good pass by, the bad ones fall.

I wish I could sleep. Sleep. The good go away.

Where are you going?

I'm on my way.

On your way where?

Things to do.

Things to do?

Yes.
They can wait.
No.
There's no hurry.
Oh yes, there is.
Stay here.
No.
They're watching me.
Don't be afraid.
They're digging their way through to me.
Don't worry.
They're not in the ditch any more.
What do I care?
They're gnawing at me.
They are dying of you.
Yes, dying of me. I've got to sleep.

A VOICE. Moo-oo-oo . . .

Cries from outside. A confusion of excited voices.

VOSS. Anna! Anna!

INA. There's one . . .

KARL. Anna . . . quick . . .

HENRY. He's drowning . . .

ANNA *flings the door open.*

ANNA. What's the matter?

INA. In the river, Anna. In the river.

ANNA. Move aside! Get out of my way, you scum!

ANNA *runs panting; she is heard jumping into the river.*

VOSS. Too late. She'll never get him out.

INA. He's gone under.

KARL. He's made it.

HENRY. Good man.

INA. Over there . . . look.

KARL. I can't see anything.

INA. Two heads.

HENRY. Only one . . .

INA. Two heads . . .

ANNA. Hey, come here.

VOSS. One more in the net.

ANNA. Come and help me, will you.

Drag him up to the field.

Get the lantern, you useless idiot!

KARL. Yes, Anna.

ANNA. Give me a hand, Henry, Voss . . .

ANNA *is heard helping the man out of the water.*

Look at the size of him. At least fourteen stone. Don't
stand around . . .

Hold on, Voss . . . and you, Henry, and now . . . one, two
. . . stand him on his head. On his head. Hold the lantern
higher. Good. Now lay him on his belly. Lord, just look
at the size of him.

VOSS. Six foot six.

ANNA. Artificial respiration. Let's go.

One two, one two.

He's still breathing . . .

One two, one two . . .

Get those dead fish out of him.

INA. They're coming up.

VOSS. Swallowed too many sardines.

KARL. Sardines. They're still alive – and wriggling.

ANNA. One two, one two.

HENRY. Watch out. He's throwing up.

ANNA. Don't vomit up your stomach. You're going to need it

KARL. Poor devil. Pretty soon you'll be lying with us in the
ditch.

ANNA. Shut up. Everybody take an arm or leg. Bring him in
to my fire.

They carry him into ANNA's *hut. The sound of feet sloshing
in the mud.*

HENRY (*sings*). Another one coming to Anna's,

Oh, what a great big fish!

ANNA. Leave him there. I'll attend to the rest.

INA. Can't I stay a while? I'm cold.

ANNA. Beat it, you slut.

VOSS. Just to warm my hands.

ANNA. Put them in your pockets.

KARL. A little piece of bread.

ANNA. Get out, I said. At the double.

HENRY. It's raining.

ANNA. I've got more important things to worry about.

INA. You're an evil woman, Anna.

ANNA. There'll be bread tomorrow morning. Now I want
peace and quiet. Back to your ditch.

He's a big fish all right. Look at that nose.

That's the right kind of nose.

Get away. You're sucking the warmth out of him.

Get out, I say.

> *The four of them go out.* ANNA *shuts the door. The chat-
> tering of the man's teeth is heard. He groans.*

ANNA. There. Now we're alone. First let's dry your clothes.

Don't lie there so stiff, you fool, you're alive.

Here, slip into this coat. It's too small. Doesn't matter.
The colour's come back to your cheeks. That's a good sign.

What's your name?

KELLY. Kelly.

ANNA. You were going downstream fast, Kelly.

KELLY. Why?

ANNA. Because the current is in a hurry. That's why.

Why I pulled you out?

What falls from the bridge belongs to me.

KELLY. I jumped.

ANNA. You fell. Nobody jumps. They only slip.

KELLY. I didn't slip. I jumped.

ANNA. Don't lie. You didn't jump. You lost your balance like
everybody else.

KELLY. No.

ANNA. You go walking along straight ahead and you think
everything's in balance, your left arm no longer than your
right and your head exactly in the middle. You're obsessed
with balance, and just when you think your balance is
perfect, your left hand hangs down lower than your right
and your neck leans to one side. One leg gives way, the
second gets shorter and down you go. But if you don't get
trapped under water, you bob up again. And start howling
at God.

Pause.

But God is old, He's fast asleep. He doesn't take off his
nightgown. He doesn't button up his trousers and run down
to the water. He's stopped caring. He leaves the fallen to
His Anna Laub.

KELLY. It's cold.

ANNA. Come closer to the fire. Your clothes are almost dry.
Here's some bread and butter ... and a piece of cheese.
The soup will be hot in a minute. Eat as much as you
can. A cold bath, coming suddenly like that, makes a man
hungry.

Knocking on the tin wall. Voices from outside.

VOSS. I'm hungry.

ANNA. Go away, Voss ... what are you doing?

Lie down.

VOSS. I'm starving.

KARL. We're all starving.

They all knock very loudly.

INA. And we're cold.

ANNA. Damn you, you ungrateful scum.

I've saved your lives.

HENRY. Nobody asked you to.

ANNA. For the thousandth time, Henry, what do you want of
me? Go home.

INA. I haven't any home.

VOSS. My people think I'm dead.

HENRY. They threw me out long ago.

ANNA. There's a doss-house in town.

KARL. Don't send us away. You saved us, Anna.

ANNA. I must have been out of my mind. If you jump again,
I promise you I won't hear a thing.

And now be quiet . . . I'm in conference.

Short pause.

KELLY. Who was that?

ANNA. Scum. Vultures . . . I can't get rid of them. They cling
to me like lice. Once you've taken pity on such creatures,
you never get rid of them.

KELLY. You'll soon be rid of me. When I leave here, you'll
never see me again. I'm different.

ANNA. That's what they all say, and then they all come back
like ants to sweet wood.

What, I ask you, is so sweet about me?

KELLY. I'll be leaving in the morning. Another two
hours . . .

ANNA. There's no hurry, Kelly. You'll stay with me by the
fire.

KELLY. No, Anna Laub.

ANNA. Yes, I say. You'll stay. I need somebody like you,
somebody to protect me.

KELLY. Not me. I've never protected anybody; never anybody but myself. Thirty-nine years – too long.

ANNA (*threatening*). You're going to stay here.

KELLY. I'm going away.

ANNA. You're not going anywhere.

KELLY. Give me my clothes.

ANNA. You're staying right here, you dog. I've saved your
life.

KELLY. It makes me sick to think of it.

ANNA. Not one step.

KELLY *goes to the door.*

KELLY. I'm going.

ANNA. Close that door. Stop.
   Pause.
   I'll beat you to a pulp, Kelly.
      She beats him. KELLY *cries out with pain.*
   Scream away. That's fine. Do you still want to leave?
KELLY (*wearily*). I want to leave.
      ANNA *strikes him again.*
ANNA. Had enough?
KELLY (*whimpering*). I want to go away.
ANNA. You're staying here.
KELLY. Yes.
ANNA. And you'll help me?
KELLY. Yes.
ANNA: And protect me?
KELLY. Yes.
ANNA. Swear it.
KELLY. I swear.
ANNA (*cries out*). Anna has a man. Anna isn't alone any more
   Music, water, wind, whistling.
INA. Voss . . .
VOSS. Yes, Ina . . .
INA. It looks bad.
VOSS (*imitating* ANNA). Your left arm gets longer than your
   right. Your right leg gives way.
INA. Don't.
VOSS (*imitating* ANNA). What falls off the bridge belongs to
   me.
INA. He's in with her by the fire.
KARL. It can't go on like this. He'll eat everything up.
INA. He's lying in there by the fire.
HENRY. Warming his bones.
KARL. And we're out here in the cold.
VOSS. She won't keep him.
INA. She'll keep him.
VOSS. He's giving in now because he wants his soup.

HENRY. Karl says it can't go on like this. What are we waiting
   for?

ANA. Sh-sh. She'll hear us.

VOSS. You mustn't talk like that.

ANA. Karl, Henry, Voss – you're men. If you don't do something soon, it will be too late.

KARL. A tin hut is better than a ditch.

VOSS. She fished us out of the water.
   Silence.

ANA. Out of the water, yes . . .

KARL. Out of the water and into the rain.

ANA. Voss, you talk to her.

VOSS. I talk and talk and talk.

KARL. Talking isn't enough. You've got to threaten her.

HENRY. Remember, we're four against one.
   We'll cut her up into little pieces. And to make sure there's
   nothing left, we'll eat her.
   *Silence. The next sentences are spoken at such feverish
   speed they can scarcely be understood.*

KARL. What?

HENRY. We'll eat everything but her shoes.

VOSS. We'll stuff her neck with corn.

ANA. We'll roast her breasts.

KARL. We'll salt her loins.

HENRY. We'll pickle her tongue.

ANA. Her cheeks . . .

KARL. . . . Her eyes . . .

HENRY. Her liver . . .

VOSS. Her heart. My heart pounds when I think of it. She
   saved us.

ANA. It gives me a tightening in the chest.

KARL. Night in my eyes.

HENRY. Sick in my entrails.

KARL. I've got to think, think.
   Ha . . . I know.

We'll weight her neck with a stone,
The stone will sink to the bottom . . .

HENRY. She'll throw the stone in your face.

Laughter.

KARL. Ha, I've got it.

The abutment. On the lowest rung of the iron ladder,
rope, a strong knot . . .

VOSS. You're good at knots.

KARL. I know them all. And they hold.

A rope . . .

INA. She'll pull the bridge down on you.

Laughter.

KARL. Pull the bridge down? How?

Think, think.

My brain must think.

VOSS. It gave up long ago.

INA. Burn her . . . to a crisp.

VOSS. That's a sin. I won't stand for it.

KARL. No choice, Voss, we have no choice.

HENRY. When?

INA. Sleep . . . sleep. Where are you going, Voss?

VOSS. I can't sleep. It leaves me no peace.

I look at you . . . at myself . . . what are we?

Ragged shadows, cold frozen meat.

When it's hot, we smell. If we're lucky, we'll end up in
the saucepans of the poor. Three mouthfuls of salty mush.
That's what we are.

INA. Sh-sh . . . don't talk. Hurry. You've got the shoes.

VOSS. Four feet and two shoes.

Two bottoms in one pair of trousers.

One coat for three . . . and a scarf for us all . . .

What are we waiting for?

KARL. Think. We must think it all out.

I'm waiting for thought. I'm thinking of thought. I'm
always thinking of thought and thoughts. The more I think

86286

the more thoughts I've got. I think them all ... every single one. And when the air is still and there's a little sun, I think ... the unthinkable. What beautiful thoughts! Unthinkable thoughts are the best!

INA. But what do you actually think, Karl?

KARL. Actually one shouldn't think at all.

But *I* think everything.

VOSS. I know what you think, Karl. You think we'll simply bash her skull in.

All cry out in horror.

Her skull, that's right ... With a board.

INA. You're a monster, Voss.

For two years I've been living in the same shoes with you, for two years we've been living in the same trousers together. For two years we've been swopping lice, but I never knew that evil was so close to me.

VOSS. What do you think, Henry?

HENRY. Peas and beans, white beans and green beans, black beans and kidney beans ... bean salad. Salad, carrots, spinach, cauliflower. All nicely prepared.

KARL. And meat.

HENRY. No meat.

There are nuts, carrots, potatoes and corn.

They grow out of the earth. There's everything in the earth. Good things come straight out of the earth, without turning corners. Animals too have eyes and ears. Don't let animals bleed to death. God made them all. The louse and the hippopotamus, the pig and the cow, they all have eyes and ears. That's why we must stick to beetroot and red cabbage, asparagus and tomatoes. But as for Anna we must bash her skull in.

INA. She leaves us out here to rot in the rain.

HENRY. She gives with one hand and takes away with the other. Gives us air and takes away our life.

KARL. There's a doss-house in town.

HENRY. While Anna lives, there's no doss-house in town for me.

KARL. You want to go to the doss-house, Henry?

INA. For old women there's an old people's home.

HENRY. Not time for that yet.

INA (*angrily*). Nobody dares to lift a finger against her. She's a man, that woman.

KARL. You mean she has a man.

INA. She doesn't need one.

VOSS. All I need is a board.

INA. Take a dozen, it won't do you any good.

VOSS. You sleep in my sleeves,
    You breathe into my mouth and
    I still can't stand you.

INA. A dozen boards won't help . . .

VOSS (*menacing*). What I can lift I can also drop.

HENRY. A board is harder than a head, Ina.

KARL. A head is only a container for small intestines.

INA (*angrily, in a loud voice*). Nobody's going to bash Anna's head in.

HENRY. Why not?

INA. Because . . . because she won't let you.
    Oppressed silence.

KARL. And suppose one waits with a board and another cries out for help, and the night is pitch dark?

HENRY. Who's going to cry out for help?

KARL. I don't have to drink the whole river. One mouthful will do.

INA. A head isn't a board.

VOSS. Exactly, you idiot.

INA. So I'm an idiot, am I? And suppose she comes trotting down and you call out for help, and you strike, and in five minutes it's all over? Then what?

HENRY. Exactly. Suddenly it's all over. That kind of death is the quickest thing in the world. Ina is right. For five years I've tortured myself with the thought of it and five years are a long time. Five years are 500,000 minutes. Each minute I wished her a thousand deaths; do you expect me to make her a present of all that in ten minutes?

NA. What *do* you want?

HENRY. She's got to live her death.

KARL. What have you got in mind?

HENRY. To warn her.

VOSS (*menacing*). You want to warn her, you dirty skunk!

HENRY. Yes, warn her. That's right. First she's got to die of fear. The rest is only a flick of the wrist.

VOSS. Right. The rest is only a flick of the wrist.

Fade out. Music, sounding like a long drawn-out 'Hooo . . .'
leads over to ANNA *and* KELLY.

ANNA. When I'm gone, Kelly, you'll have to save them.

KELLY. I can't swim.

ANNA. I couldn't either.

KELLY. And I don't want to save people. I don't want to save anybody.

ANNA. But you must. You must.

KELLY. Let them all drown . . .

ANNA. That's no way to talk.

KELLY. It's the way I talk.

ANNA. You won't talk that way for long.

KELLY. You wanted me to protect you.

All right. And now you want me to save them. You want too much.

ANNA. I know what I want.

KELLY. So did I. I wanted to drown, Anna, drown, and not see any more or hear any more. I didn't succeed. And you're to blame.

ANNA. That's an old story. I need you. You've been with me for almost three days. I threw out the others after three hours.

KELLY. I would have gone . . .

ANNA. You would have gone if . . . if I'd have let you go, bu I didn't.

KELLY. You think I haven't the strength to tear myself awa from you? You think your fire is paradise?

ANNA. It's the only one you know. Don't contradict me now You will swim and you'll save them, Kelly.

KELLY. Yes, Anna.

ANNA. That's settled. It will use up your strength . . . Rheu matism will corrode your joints, and in winter the water i cold.

KELLY. And in the ditch the animals will wait for me.

ANNA. Exactly, Kelly.

That's how it will be . . . all your life.

Here, stretch out. Take the fur.

I've got my coat. Sleep well. Tomorrow's another day.

Music.Knocking, becoming louder and menacing.

HENRY (*from outside*). Is a certain Anna Laub in there? We'v come to get her.

KELLY. Did you hear that?

ANNA. Answer him.

KELLY. Get the hell out of here. Nobody's getting anybody.

ANNA. That's right.

VOSS. Anything to eat in there? Something wrapped up i long trousers?

ANNA. What's the answer to that one?

KELLY. Get out of here before I wrap something aroun your neck.

ANNA. Not bad.

INA. Anna, Anna, you'll soon be done for.

KARL. You're nothing but an idea that will soon be forgotten

KELLY. An idea that will leave a few scars . . . which yo won't forget.

Short pause.

HENRY. Be careful, Anna. You haven't an hour to live. Whe

the last of them up there has crossed the bridge and the city sleeps, it will be your turn. Your head will go crack. Crack, crack, crack! Are you afraid?

ANNA. Afraid? What's that?

KELLY. Anna has me!

ANNA. That's right, Kelly.

INA. You bloated fish, forget about that woman. You belong to us.

KELLY. Wrong. I'm here to protect Anna.

INA. It will all be over in an hour.

HENRY. For five years I've been waiting for this evening. May the Lord protect you.

KELLY. He is asleep. But Kelly's on his toes. And now clear out of here. Move on!

KARL. I dare you to come out . . . you traitor.

> KELLY *pulls the door open and goes out. Louder music and drums.*

KELLY. I'm coming out. I'm coming.

Where are you, you bastards . . . I can't see anything.

KARL. I'm right here beside you.

KELLY. Come here. I'll kill you.

Music. Drum beats. Then decrescendo.

ANNA (*close to the microphone*). Bite them. Hit them where you can. (*More calmly.*) Choke them out of the darkness. If you can.

Music, loud laughter.

KELLY. Where are you? You scum!

Music, laughter. Then decrescendo.

ANNA (*close to the microphone*). I've brought an idiot back into this world.

Fists and no brain. You tell him to hit and he hits; he chases shadows in the dark. A madman . . .

I, Anna, am protected by . . . madness, by the madness of water, the madness of compassion with creatures, sweet wood, foul smell, the madness whose name is Kelly. The

madness whose name is fear and compassion and big fists . .
is the ruin of this country.

He's running around out there shouting. What is he shouting
about?

Music. Laughter.

KELLY. Where are you, you bastards? Come closer, I dare
you. Cowards. Just tell me where you are.

KARL. Cuckoo.

INA. Cuckoo.

KELLY. All right, cuckoo. Come here. Where are you?
Bastards, murderers, give me your necks and I'll choke
you.

KARL. Cuckoo.

VOSS. Here I am, here I am.

KELLY. Where's here?

VOSS. Still right beside you.

KELLY. Didn't I just knock your head off?

HENRY. That was my head.

KELLY. Here's something for it.

HENRY (*screams, then laughs*).

KELLY (*furious*). Stop laughing, you dog.

All laugh. Music; the music dies down.

ANNA (*close to the microphone*). He's calling them! He's
calling from his heart, from his paralysed brain. He doesn't
know reality any more. Do I?

Wasn't it a dream?

He weighed fourteen stone, none of them weighed that
much before, a man of iron. How could I, an old woman,
force him to do anything?

'Yoo-hoo!' he yelled. 'Yes,' he said, and 'I swear it.'

A man like that doesn't surrender to an old woman. Did I
really save six hundred? It can't be true. It was a lie. *I have
fished my death out of the water.*

Kelly is a drowned man.

Ice grows out of the sea and milk cows drift on the floes,

they bellow for food and their udders are bursting. My nets are torn. Dance floors for the young.

The feet move, graceful figures emerge from the fire. I'm cold.

(*She cries out*): Kelly, stay where you are!

KELLY *runs panting into the hut.*

Anna Laub is going to deliver her funeral oration.

KELLY. No speeches, this is serious, Anna Laub. There are four of them. It's pitch-dark, my fists aren't getting me anywhere. Give me your sickle. I'll make a rain of blood.

ANNA (*wearily*). There it is. Take it.

KELLY. Give me the whetstone.

ANNA. Here's the stone.

KELLY (*whetting the sickle*). Right and left, right and left. The cries will die in their throats, left and right, left and right. Blood will fall like warm rain on the field.

ANNA. Warm rain dries into bread, blood isn't rain.

KELLY. What's the matter, Anna? What has moved you? You're their net. They're your animals. If we don't butcher them, they'll kill you and who'll save the next ones?

ANNA. Too many have fallen to the fishes. I don't like corpses. If they're not alive any more, I leave them in the water.

KELLY. Nothing will be alive . . . left and right, right and left. The field will be mown down.

ANNA. Stop, stop. Stay here. When you're out there, I'm afraid.

KELLY. And when I'm with you?

ANNA. I'm afraid. Better go.

KELLY. I'll cut their eyes out.

ANNA (*imploring*). Eyes look for keels.

KELLY. Hands reaching out for you will turn to stone.

ANNA. Stone hands feel the ground, groping for a ladder to climb out of the depths. All of them want to return.

KELLY. But let them drown first. You've lost your courage.

ANNA. I don't need it any more. You have it now.

KELLY. I don't understand you.

ANNA. Nothing, nothing . . .

KELLY. Talk louder

ANNA. Nothing.

KELLY. Nothing is nothing.

> KELLY *flings the door open. Music, noise, drums.*
> *Voices in chorus repeat:* 'Anna Laub, we are coming.'
> *During the following dialogue they fade into the background.*

Do you hear them?

Outside the termites are marching, outside reality is thundering to split your eardrums.

ANNA (*softly*). And here inside is death.

(*More loudly.*) It's ghosts you hear outside. Nothing but ghosts.

KELLY. And the noise?

ANNA. What noise?

KELLY. Are you deaf? Those battle cries.

Don't you hear them?

ANNA. They're begging for forgiveness.

KELLY. They're threatening you.

ANNA. What are they saying?

KELLY. Anna Laub, we're coming.

ANNA. Coming to thank me.

KELLY. Anna, they're coming to get you.

ANNA. To take me to a celebration.

KELLY. Coming to murder you.

ANNA. Who wants to murder me?

KELLY. The termites.

ANNA. There aren't any termites. Only poor fools who wanted to die . . . and I wouldn't let them die.

(*Passionately.*) I fished them out of the water and in the end I fished out my death. Yet there's nothing sweet about me.

KELLY. I've sworn it. I'll protect you.

ANNA. Leave me alone. I'm going to deliver my funeral oration.

KELLY. They're coming, Anna. Here they are.

ANNA (*softly*). Don't come too close.

KELLY. I'm coming out.

Sound of the door, screaming, running, music. All very loud, then fading out during ANNA's *monologue.*

ANNA. In this cold, under the bridge by the river, where everything comes to an end, Anna, too, met her end. Here, in this place where everything ends, the river leads to the new country.

The music ends.

A country without cities, without tortures, a country where no one dies. White oxen, people in bright colours. Festive. Each bringing gifts. Marvellous things, radiant glories, baskets full of food on the backs of small donkeys. The house has no windows or walls.

I am the festival, the white of the oxen, the bright colours, the gifts, the glitter of glory, the marvellous things and the basket. The donkey, the white ox, and one among many. Carrying gifts with others, marvellous things and no longer alone. The people themselves are the glittering glory. *This* is the country. Now. I am the country where no one dies. Which no one can avoid and no one can enter. It has no borders, it leads nowhere and nothing leads to it, only this river, flowing cold under this bridge, the river where everything that has a beginning must end. Here the cattle bellow where they should be still. Here ragged figures carry baskets full of stones, with which they build houses. Houses with windows to seal off the world with its festivals and glories. Impalpable, uncanny, inaudible spectres, they go about their work, and you don't look until a blackness seeps through the cracks in the floor and a thin voice cries 'Help!' I feel sick.

KELLY (*far away*). Help! Help!

ANNA. There's another.

VOICE (*far away*). Help, mother.

ANNA. There's another crying out. They're in a hurry, they never succeed. (*She cries out.*) No one must escape. I'm coming.

ANNA *rushes out, slams the door. Music. The sound of* ANNA's *panting as she runs.*

I'm coming. I'm coming.

KELLY. Help. Help.

ANNA. Is it you, Kelly, my saviour?

KELLY. They're murdering me.

VOSS. Get away, Anna. It's his turn first.

Fighting. The drums take up the motif of the blows.

INA. Here's one from me.

HENRY. You asked for it.

KARL. With a sickle, eh? Here, you dog.

ANNA. Where are you, Kelly?

KELLY. Here. Here.

ANNA. Where does it hurt?

KELLY. All over.

ANNA. Can you hear me ... ?

KELLY *whimpers.*

Why did you get mixed up with them?

Leave him alone, you murderers.

He belongs to me. I'll protect you, Kelly.

Music, fighting, noise, at the climax drums.

ANNA *utters a last long drawn-out scream. Then quiet.*

VOSS. I feel sorry for her.

KARL. A weak old woman dies quickly.

HENRY. It's too bad.

INA. Really unfortunate.

KELLY. What are you going to do with me?

VOSS. With you? Are you still alive?

Where does it hurt?

KELLY. All over.

INA. There's bandage at Anna's.

HENRY. You're in bad shape.

KARL. I'll help you up.

KELLY. Is she dead?

INA. It happened so fast. She was beyond saving.

HENRY. You're bleeding.

KELLY. A man like me can't be forced. Anyone who jumps
tomorrow stays in the river. The river will wash them away.

Hunger

CHARACTERS

KARNAK
AMRAN
PANNA
THE PRINCE
THE COUNT

A large hall. A castle. Soft flute music is heard from the distance.
It comes closer. A Bach sonata for flute.

KARNAK. Amran! Amran!
The flute playing grows louder.
No, that's loud enough.
The flute goes on playing.
Good, That's just right.
(*Suddenly.*) Stop! I've had enough.
The music breaks off in the middle of a note.
AMRAN. Enough? If you say so. Enough for me in any case.
I like to play and I like to stop. I make no demands. If you
say, Amran, play, I play; if you say, Amran, stop . . .
KARNAK (*interrupts him*). Stop. Stop. My ears. My ears are
grottoes. Every word has a triple echo. My head is a room,
bigger than this one, as big as a universe, my head is a
universe without a cover. A head is as big as a universe and
as empty – every word, every clearing of the throat becomes
a trumpet, cudgels belabouring my skin.
A scratching is heard, then a whirring greatly amplified,
then loud electronic noises.
An ocean of noise. That's what I am. Weight: sixty-five,
age: sixteen stone – almost. A fat, sick man. My heart is
tired. My lungs are on strike. My eyes are bad, my ears
are bad . . . my stomach is empty . . . it's not a stomach . . .
something empty . . . called a stomach, feels no food . . .
a vacuum, it doesn't feel anything . . . This vacuum has no
feeling for food. Amran, play.
AMRAN continues playing where he broke off. KARNAK
speaks, very lively.
Bring me glass, Panna, and a mortar . . .
PANNA. A mortar?

KARNAK. Quick, a mortar. Now you're going to see something.

AMRAN. Wood and stone and glass. I've seen everything.

KARNAK. Glass is neither stone nor wood. Glass goes into the blood. Tears a man apart, cuts open his veins. From inside. That's glass.

PANNA (*brings the mortar*). Here's the mortar.

KARNAK. Put it down, Panna. And now watch. Sit down.

Glass is splintered in the mortar.

Grind it fine, very fine, but not too fine. That's right.

PANNA. I've got an electric machine for that, Mr Karnak.

KARNAK. A machine? We have a machine for it? You should have brought it.

PANNA (*singing in recitative*). I have a machine in the kitchen, my machine grinds fine, very very fine, my machine in the kitchen, my wonderful brand-new machine. I can grind anything in it, until everything turns to liquid. My beautiful machine in the kitchen, my wonderful machine – you've never seen one like it before.

KARNAK (*impatiently*). Go and get it . . .

(PANNA *goes out. To* AMRAN.) Liquid glass. Imagine. We have a machine that grinds glass to water. That's just the thing. After glass leather, after leather iron. If our machine grinds everything, it must also . . .

PANNA. Here it is, Mr Karnak.

KARNAK. Does it grind iron?

PANNA. You said glass before.

KARNAK. Yes, yes, of course. I'm only asking. Does it grind iron?

PANNA (*with voluptuous pleasure*). My special machine, my darling machine grinds everything, everything, everything . . . so it must grind iron.

The glass is poured from the mortar into the machine.

KARNAK. That will do for a start. My question was purely theoretical. I hope I still have a right to ask . . .

PANNA (*with servile zeal*). Oh, of course, Mr Karnak, forgive me, I didn't mean ... Ask anything you please, you don't even have to ask, just speak. A master speaks, asking is beneath him. I ask, Amran asks ... but when the master speaks, we are silent.

KARNAK. Which button?

PANNA. This one, Mr Karnak.

KARNAK (*presses a button. The sound of an electric coffee mill, only somewhat louder*). It works fast. Look how fast it works! Damp, it's getting damp! Glass has turned to water. (*He drinks.*) Amran, your health! Panna, your health! (*He drinks again.*) Your health! Amran, how about a few dozen bottles?

AMRAN. If that is your wish.

KARNAK. It is Karnak's wish. I am Karnak. A. L. Karnak, a Biblical king. Born in humble circumstances. In filth. But now I am the great Karnak. My wish is law.

A factory. The sound of enormous machines. The words must be heard over the noise.

PRINCE. Once more, Count. One more load will be enough. Splendid.

A great sound of falling glass. Steps passing the machines. The sounds change into the gushing of a waterfall.

How much does it come to, Count?

COUNT. Twenty-five thousand gallons, Prince. Could be a few gallons more.

PRINCE. Could be, means should be. How much does it actually come to?

COUNT. Twenty-five thousand gallons, one quart and three gills.

PRINCE. Why didn't you tell me that in the first place? A modest output, but we'll keep on working.

Factory whistle, voices and footsteps of workers. Machines are turned off. The voices of a large crowd.

PRINCE (*the resonance of an enormous room accompanies his*

voice). Friends! Associates! Workers! At the end of this first day of work I wish to communicate to you men and women, workers and office personnel of the Karnak Glass Processing Works, my heartfelt thanks and those of our honoured master, who, I regret to say, cannot be present today because he is planning new and larger factories. (*Thunderous applause.*) We can be proud of this day's achievement. From sixty thousand gallons at noon, our production rose by five-thirty to a hundred and fifty thousand ... (*Loud applause and cries of* 'Hurrah!') That was our first day. I am confident that in ten years we shall have gathered, crushed and liquefied all the existing glass in the country ... (*Loud* 'Hurrah's!) Our plan calls for the utilization of other substances, and I assure you that we will not rest until all existing raw materials ... (*Cries of* 'Hurrah!', 'Three cheers for Karnak.')

KARNAK. Amran, glass ... glass is tasteless. Iron is insipid, copper tastes like cod liver oil, and jewels are no less tasteless than the pink lemonade they gave me as a child ...

AMRAN. Yes, Mr Karnak. That's how it is with hunger. Eating doesn't help. We've seen that. I couldn't even list all the materials you have consumed in the last few years.

KARNAK (*roars like an animal*). Hunger! Hunger!

AMRAN (*also roars*). Enough! Enough!

KARNAK (*more calmly*). If the sun were to rise thirty times a day, if rivers were to flow uphill, if mountains danced and cities sank into the earth, everything would still be the same.

AMRAN. What can we do for you, Mr Karnak? I can't stand it any longer. How about words?

KARNAK. What?

AMRAN. Words.

KARNAK. I thought you said curds. I had three bowls full this afternoon.

AMRAN. Not curds, words. I'll make up a big word for you. If you don't like it, I'll make up another, and so on. How about akalapuntikandurapeitikank. Served cold. It's Eskimo.

KARNAK. Not so fast. What was that again? I lost track.

AMRAN. Akalapuntikandurapeitikank.

KARNAK (*writes it down and repeats*). Akalapuntikandurapeitikank. I've got it. How should I take it?

AMRAN. Cold. As is.

KARNAK. No sauce?

AMRAN. No sauce. As is.

KARNAK (*tears up the paper, puts it in his mouth: chewing*).
Not bad. In fact it's good. That's a good word. It tastes
good.

AMRAN. Now a whole sentence.

KARNAK. In English?

AMRAN. Nutritious in any language. Here it is: 'That which
is infinite by definition contains within it the finiteness which
is its antithesis, but of this unity the former is the essence.'

KARNAK (*repeats the sentence, smacking his lips*). 'That which
is infinite by definition contains within it the finiteness
which is its antithesis, but of this unity the former is the
essence.' Hm. I've got it. Not bad. Old, but one doesn't
notice it. That was a good appetizer. Have you any more?

AMRAN. Here's another: 'Its essence which is pure as-suchness is so vitiated by the admixture of a quality that it
becomes a finitized infinity.'

KARNAK. Sounds odd. But maybe there's something in it.
I'll try it. (*He repeats the sentence, seems to like it but belches
in the end.*) 'Its essence which is pure as-suchness is so
vitiated by the admixture of a quality that it becomes a
finitized infinity.' Well, not quite what I was hoping for.
Not bad. Not good. Flat. Not enough seasoning. Too
sweet. Give me something strong. Something heavier. A
man's food. No more pudding.

AMRAN. Karnak who, devouring the world, gags as he chews,
to raise whose dough the air is not sufficient, Karnak, a
clod who lives only because he was born and doesn't die

because he hasn't the breath to expire, who hour by hour chokes on his greed though in perfect health, whom one tries to feel sorry for, but fails. Mongol, moron, idiot, who in other countries would have been exterminated long ago, but who in this country lives on and on, waiting for a new hero to destroy him, who eats, eats, eats, but is never full. Kill him, kill Karnak the monster. (*Screaming.*) Destroy him.

KARNAK (*after a brief pause during which the words fade away, calmly and gravely*). I don't care for that. It's inelegant. It's personal. And in bad taste. Don't you think so?

AMRAN (*hysterically*). Stop. Stop. (*More calmly, but still violently.*) That's enough! I've had enough of you! (*He gasps for air.*) Here's your flute, make your own music. I won't play for you any more. Let me go. I'm through.

KARNAK (*with serene superiority*). I'm a practical man. If you don't want to play for me any more, don't play for me; if you don't want to work, don't work. Do what you please. You're not a slave. You're my employee. A purchased friend. Money doesn't interest you any more. You want to go? Go. I have nothing to say. No complaint. Do you see me weeping? I have nothing to offer. Only my money. I'm empty. I hate money. I'm rich. Very rich. A rich man has only one thing. (*He screams and whimpers heartbreakingly.*) Hunger! Hunger!

PANNA (*enters*). Forgive the interruption, Mr Karnak, but I've just prepared this for you . . . a new recipe . . . something really very new. Won't you please . . . it's something very special . . . I hope you enjoy it.

KARNAK. Put it down, you silly goose, you cackle as if . . . Good Lord . . . as if you really had something to offer. Probably something to eat. (*He sits down, lifts the lid.*) No! It can't be! My goodness. Very nice. Very original. A flea? A flea in aspic? Is that it? Liquid? Ah, a flea in water. (*He laughs.*) Excellent. (*He drinks.*) There. That was fun.

Now we've had a flea in water. Ha ha! A tiny animal, ha ha, inside the gigantic Karnak. Ha ha! (*Suddenly sulking.*) But it doesn't help. It doesn't help at all. Even the tiniest flea, Panna, doesn't help. In the end a flea is nothing but a flea. It's edible, Panna. I'm hungry for ... for something inedible.

AMRAN. You don't understand that, Panna. Nobody understands. We're all too stupid. Our master doesn't want to eat anything that's edible, but since everything is edible, he doesn't want to eat at all, and that's why he keeps screaming how hungry he is.

PANNA. I don't understand a single word.

AMRAN. But that's how it is.

PANNA. That's how it is, that's how it is. That's all I hear. That's what they said during the war. Their 'that's how it is' was so loud you couldn't hear the bombs falling. That's how it is. And all of a sudden: boom. When the houses were gone and the people too, it was the same story: that's how it is. Something has got to be done, Mr Amran. We've got to do something. It can't go on like this.

AMRAN. I'm leaving.

KARNAK. And the 'that's how it is' will stay behind. It's intolerable. Something must be done. (*Shouting.*) You're right, Panna, it can't go on like this. When I'm full, I cry hunger. But I'm never full and I cry hunger. It seems to me that I'm really hungry or I wouldn't cry hunger.

PANNA (*angrily*). How can a man be hungry when he eats all day?

KARNAK. Yes indeed, how?

PANNA. If he had no stomach. But that can't be. Or a stomach ulcer. But the doctors say you're in the best of health. Something must be wrong.

KARNAK. Something must be wrong. I eat till I can't eat any more, and I'm never full.

PANNA. There are a lot of poor people who go looking for a

crust of bread or a dish of soup, and there are poor people who find meat for their soup and a crust of bread and cry out for vegetables and fresh butter. There are some who haven't enough and can't help it, but people who have everything and eat everything and go on being hungry ... that kind of hunger does not exist. Something must be done Right away.

AMRAN (*as narrator, with a different voice*). Doctors came and went. It turned out that Karnak's hunger was symbolic From then on, Karnak, who was intelligent enough to understand this, referred to it as 'my symbolic hunger' and maintained that it was just as painful as normal hunger, if not more so.

KARNAK. I feel it. In here. It hurts. It hurts more. And there's nothing I can eat for symbolic hunger. Or if I'm only deluding myself and it's not what I think, if it's not hunger at all, then something else hurts in my stomach, something that may just as well be called hunger. A cancer perhaps, or a child, or a colic, or a pumpkin. It hurts all day and never stops.

AMRAN (*as narrator*). A phenomenon. Food for thought. We'll try a few tests. We've got to take this thing seriously. (*In his normal voice.*) I will sing you the song of the glutted.
    (*Sings.*)
The skeleton that walks erect
and commonly is known as man,
which daily nourishes its meat
and cries all day for more to eat
for himself and all his clan—
My advice to you, before it's too late, is to pin down his hands and stop his mouth. And if he resists, choke him ... now. That's it.

    A brief struggle. AMRAN *clutches* KARNAK *by the throat.* KARNAK *gasps for air.*

KARNAK. So that's what you really wanted. False feelings,

malignant thoughts, murder. So that's it. Down through the ages they've come as you have come, with songs and slogans and noble, humane feelings, to choke me. Down through the ages they've come with their guilty consciences, saying that something must be done to help me. They come to kill me. Murderers. They'd crucify me, once they almost burned me, but even I – the mad, sick Karnak, who cries hunger though he has no right to – want to cry out. I cry hunger . . . because I . . . because I'm full.

AMRAN (*as narrator*). Choking didn't help. We must find other methods. Poison perhaps.

(*In his normal voice*). Here I am again. I've come from South America. I've brought you something, a speciality. A mushroom.

KARNAK (*joyfully*). Poisonous?

AMRAN. A gram is enough to kill two hundred people.

KARNAK. Let's have it. You don't mean it. (*He eats and smacks his lips.*) A bad mushroom.

AMRAN (*frightened*). You're not dying?

KARNAK. Not so far.

AMRAN. You should have been dead long ago.

KARNAK. Me? Dead? (*He laughs.*)

AMRAN (*utterly amazed*). He's alive.

KARNAK. He's alive. Ha ha! He's alive. (*Ironically.*) No, he's not alive. I'm dead. (*He laughs.*)

AMRAN. He's dead and alive. A living corpse.

KARNAK. What difference does it make? Dead, alive. One way or another. Symbolic or not. In any case, I'm here.

AMRAN (*stuttering*). Good God, perhaps . . . my eyes deceive me and you're an angel . . . not a man. But if you're not a man and your body is only the shell, then perhaps it can be defeated, then everything is different. Metaphysically speaking, it's different.

KARNAK. Panna, my second breakfast!

The table bell merges into the ringing of large and small

church bells. A chorus of monks sings a Latin prayer the words of which cannot be clearly understood.

AMRAN (*as priest in the pulpit, his voice echoes in the cathedral*) Here, my son, eat of the wood of our Saviour's cross. His blood and his spirit are in every fibre.

KARNAK (*eats and smacks his lips*). Phoo! Your holy wood tastes like rotten squid. No, it's not for me. It's nauseating

AMRAN (*as priest, accompanied by organ and choir*). Then God forgive you. If his cross is not to your liking, leave his house Go and never return.

The choir grows louder. High, angelic voices.

(*As narrator*). They excommunicated him although he didn't give a damn.

A Bach sonata for flute is heard first in the distance, then coming closer.

KARNAK. Amran! Amran! Splendid. That's fine.

AMRAN *plays more loudly, stops, and sings Purcell's 'If music be the food of love'.*

AMRAN (*sings*). If music be the food of love, play on, play on . . .

KARNAK. Stop. That's enough. Music and love and a sprinkling of words. Words that no one knows and no one believes any longer, a mere echo of things we understand in our dreams. Love and music. And then you add honour and King and Country and still more words, and you look for meaning where there is no meaning, and consolation where there is none. And conjure up past times and an entire poetry of feelings and phrases, because you wish to cure the incurable. Hunger has nothing to do with food. Even I know that. I've also tried not eating. There have been epochs when I wasn't alive, I was still stone or air, and you weren't here either to hear my lamentations, even if I had screamed.

AMRAN. I don't want to hear. I understand. Enough of your lamentations. No, I won't listen, but the noise is unbearable.

KARNAK. The poisoned cherries of my summer, the deadly nightshade we were not allowed to eat, the lethal mushrooms of my autumn that we mustn't touch, and where is the cold of my winter, against which you had to warm me? Oh, not to sleep and not to feel a thing! Belly, where are you taking me? (*Whimpering*.) Hunger!

ANNA (*tenderly*). What can I offer you? Poor man. Good man, what can I do for you? Here, take this, take everything. Drink this, drink it all. You good, dear, poor man.

KARNAK *drinks and smacks his lips.*

AMRAN (*as narrator*). Nothing helped. He drank her breast empty and every breast. Love did not appease him. He grew heavy and felt nothing. He said:

KARNAK. I do feel it. Where do I feel it? Here, I feel it here. Nothing. Here I feel nothing. In here where I feel it, there's nothing. It grows in me. Flesh. I am flesh. But I feel nothing. There's nothing there. It turns into flesh, but I feel nothing.

AMRAN. Nothing. The milk didn't help.

He'd have eaten the breast too and perhaps the woman with it.

And he wasn't sated because there was nothing in him that could be sated.

The poor man!

AMRAN (*more Bach: he speaks when the music is finished*). A year has passed. Here I am again. With my master, my god.

Here he is. What's the matter, Karnak? I didn't recognize you. You're not bellowing.

What's the matter? Where's your hunger?

KARNAK. I'm sated now. I'm full.

Full of air. My body is full of air. And full of blood. My blood is full of cells, full of everything that lives and builds and eats.

AMRAN. Karnak, I don't know you. How you talk!

KARNAK. Full of bones and sinews,
    full of entrails, full of flesh,

full of corpuscles, full of tissue. I am replete.

AMRAN. I don't understand. First you were empty, now suddenly you're full. A mystery.

KARNAK. I am a barn full of grain, a river full of water, an ocean full of salt – full of good things.

AMRAN. And you've stopped eating?

KARNAK. Yes, I'm sated, sated and full, full and fat and heavy.

AMRAN. Haven't you always been?

KARNAK. I was always empty, empty as a universe, quite empty, don't you remember?

I ate everything that was edible and I also ate what was not edible. Now I'm full. Isn't that normal?

AMRAN. Something is wrong.

KARNAK. What's wrong? I'm normal. I'm not hungry any more, only now and then like everyone else,

I eat normally like everyone else, three or four meals a day,

sometimes more, sometimes less, all perfectly normal . . .

AMRAN. I don't know what to think. In someone else I'd have found it normal,

in you it's somehow . . . not normal if you're normal . . .

Because there was this hunger that was no normal hunger . . .

KARNAK. It was and is no more.

AMRAN. It was no common hunger, it was a very special hunger. The kind you don't forget.

KARNAK. Nothing is forgotten. Only it doesn't trouble any more. I'm cured, don't you see? Salvation has come to me. Now I'm like everyone else.

In perfect health.

AMRAN. I hear you. I hear what you say and I don't know why, but it seems to me . . . that you're different and still the same. What has happened?

PANNA. It's true, Amran. It's true. I think it was a Sunday, you had just left. Mr Karnak said to me: I don't want

anything, Panna. Just like that, as you and I might say it:
I don't want anything ... and leaves his food untouched.
I don't want anything, he said. With my own ears I heard
him say it. I don't want anything. All of a sudden, for no
reason at all: I don't want anything. Why? I asked him.
How come? From one minute to the next, it was: I don't
want anything.

AMRAN. I hear you, Panna, I hear every word, but somehow
it's not right. He's the same, he hasn't lost weight ... and
he seems perfectly happy. What's going on? There's something wrong. Let me go. I've got to leave this place. Immediately.

KARNAK. Nothing, Amran, nothing is wrong. You're worrying
yourself for nothing. But one day, just before dinner, the
kitchen smell came to me. It smelled of dead animals, of
trampled, decayed blossoms, of compost, of poisonous
flowers. The kind that grow in my own garden. First came
the smell, then the food. Corpses. My stomach turned. So
many dead things – I couldn't touch it.

AMRAN. Strange. You always used to eat.

KARNAK. Not just dead ... oh no. A disgusting deadness.
A death that befouls everything. I am still sick, but the pain
in my stomach, the hunger is gone. Whether I eat the world
or not, Amran, doesn't matter any more.

AMRAN. Well, if you're really happy, if everything is as it
should be and you're at peace ...

KARNAK. A man like every other, Amran. A man among men.
Disgust did it. Disgust cured me. Disgust ... the poison
cherries of my summer, the bad mushrooms of my autumn,
the cold death of my winter. It wasn't easy.

AMRAN. What's the matter, Karnak? What's wrong?

PANNA. The master is tired. Let him sleep.

AMRAN. Tired? Karnak tired?

PANNA. The master is dead, Amran. Dead. Our dear, good
Mr Karnak suddenly died one Sunday afternoon. Panna,

he cried out, Panna, I don't, I don't want any more. (*She weeps.*) And he was no more. That was the Sunday after you went away. You went on a Friday, you deserted him. Deserted and betrayed him.

AMRAN. What kind of man is it who talks when he's dead? What kind of man is it who devours the world when he's alive? Tell me, Panna. What is the smell that brings disgust?

PANNA (*sobbing*). You made music, you fed him words, you gave him sentences. I gave him . . . fleas. (*She weeps.*) Then you went away and he was alone. His hunger left him and . . . he passed away.

The final chorus of the St Matthew Passion.

Fear

CHARACTERS

A
B
C } Men
D
E

F   A woman

M   A doctor

K 1 } Children
K 2

SCENE ONE

Music, at first 'Tibetan' and 'mysterious' forest music (brass and woodwind), becoming tender, and romantic. One hears successively the croaking of frogs, the howling of a wolf, steps through the underbrush, a breaking of branches. The song of a lark, then a prolonged twittering.

A. Hey, you ... Birdman, stop that noise. This is a forest. A sanctuary of nature. If you want to sing around here, you've got to have wings.

B *(chirps a few notes)*. If you don't like it, I'll sing something else.

A. Never mind. The birds are enough for me.

B. I've got to practice. I'm rehearsing for the world bird impersonation championship in Brussels next year. Last year in Paris I took third prize, but next year ... *(He sings like a robin)* ... next year, it's got to be first prize.

A. I'd give you the first prize right now.

B. You look so gloomy. Life is fun. The doctor says so too. In the woods, he says, I'll get fresh air, good for the larynx, good for the lungs. Why don't you sing with me ?

A. How do I go about it ?

B. Breathe in and out. And in between ...
He chirps and twitters.

A. You're in a restricted area.

B. What about you ?

A. I'm sort of a forester.

B. Ah, my dear forester, why don't you give it a try ? You have a golden opportunity. You could practice all day, but you don't. I want the first prize in Brussels, not the third. Let's practice together, like this, first we'll learn the call of the jackdaw (*He does the call of the jackdaw.*) ... You don't want to? You take life too seriously, I used to be like that. I'm a happy man, a birdman. World championship for solo bird song. That's my dream. (*He chirps and twitters.*)

A. That's enough now. Where are you going?

B. Bass, mackerel, and herring, a whole basketful. (*Gaily.*) We're having a ... fish orgy (*He laughs.*) My wife is a good cook. In the evening friends are coming. We'll chirp and twitter far into the night. I'm going home, home, home. Home to my wife and children ...

A. You've got birds on the brain.

B. Home, home, home. (*He whistles.*) Going home.

A. You're getting on my nerves.

B. Because I'm a happy man.

A. I wouldn't call you a man.

B. A woodpecker and a starling were having a singing contest ... (*He twitters.*) Then the cuckoo joined in. (*Cuckoo call.*) And soon every bird in wood and meadow sang. (*He chirps and twitters like various birds.*)

A (*after a brief pause*). You make me sick.

B (*twitters and calls out merrily*). Good-bye.

> Steps are heard in the underbrush. B goes off, his bird-calls die down.

A (*in a loud voice*). Halt! Come back.

B (*comes back slowly*). Here I am. (*Forest music. Suddenly B cries out.*) Help! Help! (*Weakening.*) Help! (*Rattling.*) Help! (*Silence.*)

A. Come into the woods with me, my cart has broken down Help me up the mountain.

B (*humbly*). At your service, forester.

> Panting and coughing. Cursing between their teeth, they push the cart. B has stopped.

What have you got in there under the cover?

A. Wood. Come on now, don't stop.

B. Taking wood to the forest?

A. Wood to the forest. (*They go on pushing.*) Dead wood. Heave
... ho! That's it. Heave ho! The worst will soon be over.

B. Heave ... ho! (*He sighs with relief.*) That's better.

A. I take wood to the forest. Been doing it for years. If I didn't,
how would the wood get to the forest? Somebody's got to
put it there.

B. Is that your job?

A. My vocation.

B (*the cart is rolling faster now*). Wood to the forest. Water to
the sea. Sand to the desert. Clouds to the sky. Dead people
to the other world.

A. Somebody's got to do it. God can't do it all by himself.

B. Where are we going?

A. Till we can't go on.

B. How did you know me?

A. By the way you talk. All that stuff about your happy
home and your wife who cooks so well and your dear
children. Sounded familiar. You hate them. You hate them
all.

B. Yes and no.

A. Faster now. We want to make it up there before dark.

SCENE TWO

*In the forest. The sounds of trees being felled. Sawing. The
singing of men at work.*

B. The good life continues in another world. The good life is
gone. The good life is somewhere, not here. For three
months now we've been quarrelling. I sleep in terror under
the leaves. Forest above me, below me, whichever way I
look, wood and nothing else. Is the whole world made of
wood? Or is it only that I see nothing else? Of all my

desires only one is left. Again fear has stopped my breath. Listen to me, men. It's not too late yet.

He hammers furiously with his fist, beats his head against the wood, cries desperately.

A. Don't break my trees with your skull. Calm down. As far as they're concerned you're dead. Written off. The fish have rotted. The dishes are cleared away. Your friends are singing and drinking without you. Your children are going to school. Your wife is cooking.

B. As if nothing had happened.

A. As if nothing had happened. You're in heaven now, what more do you want? For the living you're someone who has gone away. Once you're gone, there's no further need to go away. You've got everything behind you ... almost.

B. Almost? Is there something more to come?

A. Not much. Just a little.

B (*sighing*). The good life somewhere in another world ...

A. That'll do. I know the refrain. Always the same: The good life somewhere in another world ...

B. ... it left me no time for guilt or debts ... I've always paid up, paid my bills in advance. Everything was in order.

A. Some order! A pigsty! Your good life is a disease, every bit as mortal as a bad life. It's over now. (*Sarcastically.*) You can thank your stars. The beautiful world that smells of dead fish ...

B. ... where people live happily and gather together ...

A (*laughs mockingly*). I know the stupid laughter, the stupid talk, the jostling and sweating, the moist hands on drinks.

B. ... where people gather and listen to music and talk with the voices of birds.

A (*laughs; then seriously: during his speech the same music as at the beginning of the scene, dying down in a metallic echo*). Even the music is better up here. Listen to it. Open your ears.

*He sings an improvisation on a theme from Bach, somewhere
between aria and recitative.*

Thou art in heaven, I am thy God, I have delivered thee of
thy torments.

Grief and care have passed, thine earthly life is done, thou
hast come home to the saints and to me thy God.

(*In a speaking voice.*) Did you imagine it would be like this?

B. The Devil take you with your religion and your hymn
singing! No. I expected to find eternal peace. I thought this
would be a good place to sleep. You're driving me crazy
with your singing.

A. Get to work now and no dawdling. You slept in your
mother's womb, you slept in kindergarten, you slept at
school. You have been sleeping all your life.

SCENE THREE

In the woods. Trees are being felled.

C. Don't stand around. Take hold. You are not in England.

B. It's too heavy.

D. It's no lighter for any of us. Take hold, you loafer.

E. We didn't expect this either. In heaven, I always thought,
I'll be able to drink my beer in peace.

He pants as he hauls a tree trunk.

B. In heaven, I thought, I will fly my kites, that was my dream.
But this is a penal colony. A concentration camp. This is
not what I wanted. Not at all. I was just on my way home.

D. But you didn't make it. You went too slow.

B. In heaven, I dreamed, you walk barefoot on soft sand and
swim in the clouds. That was my idea.

E. Still, the time passes more quickly – when it passes.

C. And the boss is always around.

B. He made me help him with his cart. He wanted to talk with me. First I refused, then he called me back. If I ever had any conception of heaven, I saw it as a meadow.

D. When *he* shouts halt, the grass stops growing. Why didn't you run away?

C. That's what you should have done.

E. Yes, why not?

D. Your legs must have been too short.

C. You had lead in your shoes.

B. My feet were made of lead. He caught me. Telling lies about domestic bliss. The sweet pastry didn't agree with me. I spat it up. And when I realized that wife and children and all my happiness made me sick, I tried to run away. Too late. He called me. HALT, he shouted, and that was that. Finished, washed up.

D. Who caught you?

B. He, it. Fear.

D. Fear leads everybody into the woods.

E. Whichever way you look, the glue of fear. You stick to it.

C. You should have been more careful.

B. I wanted to practice happiness. (*He chirps sadly.*) Do you understand? I always spoke in different voices. Because the noise was so terrible. Even in my mother's womb, maddening voices.

A symphony of noises increasing in tempo and volume.

Steps, bells, ships, automobiles, stamping, shooting, screaming. The pain in my throat came from the voices. The doctor said: You must go to the country and learn the language of the birds, then you won't hear the rest. For two years I was all right, I took third prize in Paris, France, and started training at once for next year in Brussels. In the middle of my work, on the threshold of success, he stopped my mouth with his Halt. Instead of first prize a heavy axe. Instead of pleasure slavery.

Steps, the crackling of underbrush. Work sounds.

D. Quick. Here comes the old man.

A. That'll do for today. No hurry. Keep on like this, men, and in nine million years the job will be done. Every tree uprooted, in every hole a new tree. Clearing and planting. It goes quickly.

B. Nine million years?

A. In a hundred years you'll be used to it. You have no choice, but plenty of time. Good night, men.

SCENE FOUR

At home. A clock ticks. Dishes are being washed. Children's laughter in the background. Popular music. Now and then a car passes.

B. Aren't you going to ask me where I've been?

F. Where have you been?

B. With those people out in the woods.

F. Did you have a good time?

B. Aren't you going to ask me why I didn't come home?

F. Why didn't you come home?

B. Because he called me back. Wouldn't let me go.

F. Called you back? Wouldn't let you go?

B. Why don't you ask me how I felt?

F. How did you feel?

B. Not good. Far from it. I thought of my family here at home. Why don't you ask me if I thought of you?

F. Did you think of us?

B. Every day, every hour.

F. You did? You thought of us? But that didn't keep you from staying away for three months?

B. I had no choice.

F. Yes, you had no choice.

B. Don't you want to know what I did out there?

F. No. I don't want to know.

B. Ask me.

F. What did you do out there?

B. Dug up trees. Lived in a hole in the ground. Don't you want to know how long it would have gone on?

F. No. I don't want to know.

B. Ask me.

F. How long would it have gone on?

B. The clearing nine million years. The planting nine million years. That's a long time. Admit it. A long time.

F. Yes, it's a long time.

B. Didn't you miss me?

F. We missed you.

B. Weren't you unhappy?

F. Yes, we were unhappy.

B. Didn't you grieve?

F. We grieved.

B. But you went on living all the same.

F. We went on living all the same. The first day I was angry. The fifth day I was sad, the tenth curious, at the end of a month worried, after two months desperate, after three months disappointed. And now you're back again.

B. Yes, now I'm back.

F. When I woke up in the empty bed, I looked for you. Then I fell asleep again and dreamed of you.

B. Where was I? Where did you see me in your dream?

F. Down here. At home. Busy. In my dream I fell asleep again. You stayed down here.

B (*excitedly*). I was up there. In the forest. With God. In eternity. In heaven. Dead. Resurrected. Here I am. With you. Alive. Here. Touch me.

F. Yes, it's you. Do you still chirp?

B. I've lost the voices, forgotten the music. Have I changed?

F (*after a short pause*). I can't see any difference. You look the same. You are the same. Maybe you were never away. Your fear is worse.

B. Nine million years are half a day. I was gone a hundred and eighty half-days.

F. One wouldn't think so.

Approaching sounds of CHILDREN. *Now they are in the room.*

K 1. There's daddy.

K 2. Where have you been, daddy?

B. In the woods.

K 2. What for?

B. Digging up trees.

K 1. And keeping us waiting.

B. I couldn't help it.

K 2. Is the work finished now?

K 1. Daddy, do a thrush.

K 2. Daddy, a blackbird, please.

B. Not now, children. That's all over for the present. Now I'm tired. I've got to rest.

F. Sleep. Take a good rest.

B. I can't sleep. Too much to do. They hide the roots, we find them. Arms clinging to arms. Get the axe. We smash the heads and cut the trunks into pieces. Who would not like to conceal the monstrous and hear no more of it? No pity for the trees, I say. A quick end to a long existence. Trees are animals without tongues, we must destroy them; our work is to make room on earth for the new man. Die, die, let them all die. In every new hole a new tree. I saw death with my own eyes; now I know what can help us all.

F. Are you talking in your sleep?

B. Do I sound as if I were talking in my sleep? I'm speaking of necessities. When death threatens us, we must *make* death. Necessity, logic, reason. I'm not asleep; I walk and talk and grow more lucid every day.

SCENE SIX

At the doctor's. Sounds of a sawmill in the background. A door is closed. The sounds stop.

M. Bring the woman in. Well, what's wrong with him?

F. He screams: This is my forest. Otherwise he scarcely speaks.

M. Aspirin.

F. At night he yells: Tear out the trunks and the roots.

M. Codein.

F. He says: We're already in heaven. We're all in heaven, he says.

M. Anadin.

F. He keeps shouting at me: I'm sane.

M. Remove his brain.

F. He won't allow it.

M. He won't notice. We'll tell him he has an abscess that must be removed, and we'll take out his brain.

F. It will hurt.

M. We'll tell him: My good man, you have an abscess that's impairing your vision.

B. I see trees.

M. In a few years you'll be blind. A sorry state for a man who wants to see his fine home, his dear wife and his clever children.

B (*absently*). Yes, yes. My clever children, my fine home . . . (*In a loud voice.*) Give me a hand instead . . . heave ho! . . . with this cart, I've got wood for the forest. That's it. Once more. Heave ho! Help me, doctor. Please help me.

M. I can help you. Eight o'clock tomorrow morning, but no breakfast, please.

SCENE SEVEN

In the woods.

A. So now you see.

B. Now I see.

A. They've removed it?

B. To prevent blindness.

A. Can you see the forest better now?

B. Now I know where I am. I see the trees.

A. Can you see what there is to be done?

B. Now I see everything.

A. You come and go as you please.

B. Now I find the way more easily. I live here and there, not here and not there, I see everything here and there.

A. Your skull is emptier now, or do looks deceive me?

B. First you took my fear, my birds' voices, the doctor took the rest. He took my brain. Now I understand everything. Now I can see nothingness, the air, the not-thought and the not-desired. Everything is clear.

A. Can you see the earth from inside as a butterfly sees itself in a larva?

B. Yes, and the bird in the egg. Words in the mouth. Blood in my own heart. The nucleus in every cell. Death in living things. Now I have time. Let them cook their own fish at home. I can see heaven and earth. Here it is. Here.

A. This isn't a forest, my friend. This is a punitive expedition, we dig up the dead and then we must bury them again.

B *(screaming)*. Liar! This is a forest.

A. Bad metaphysics makes for bad men. Even if you see all you say, you haven't seen a thing. We call it 'forest', but forest is only the beginning. After forests come stones. When the stones have been piled up to make cities, we pull them down again. After the stones – the waters. We still have all the oceans to drink. How big is your belly? After the waters, the heavens. When we've gathered in the stars, we'll stop. We've hardly begun. Take hold – both hands! That's right ... maybe it's underneath.

B. What?

A. Two thousand generations are buried here. That's an eternity. Maybe it's underneath. Take hold ...

SCENE EIGHT

At the doctor's. Same sounds as before, which fall silent when the woman closes the door.

F. Now he wants to see something new every day.

M. Baldrian.

F. He is nowhere now. Only his knocking is left.

M. Catalgin.

F. He knocks on the floor-boards.

M. Adenylocrat.

F. Without his reason he doesn't know where he is any more. He knocks all the time, he knocks and knocks. His words are blows.

M. We'll have to make a little incision and remove his heart ...

F. He won't allow it.

M. It depends on how we put it ...
   My friend, in order to avoid a possible collapse of your circulation and prevent an abortion of both ventricles, I must advise an operation of both lungs ...

B. Both lungs? That must hurt.

M. Hurt? Hurt? Breathing is extremely unwholesome – even of fresh forest air. Oxygen nourishes the blood-stream. But since yours will soon require no further nourishment, we had better remove the lungs so as to obviate unnecessary breathing. I'm the doctor, I ought to know.

B *(taps his forehead, it sounds hollow like a barrel)*. My head is hollow, but I have confidence in medicine.

He taps again, waits for an answer, and taps again.

Perhaps. It's not quite clear to me yet.

M. My good friend, tapping your skull won't help, there's nothing in it, nothing old and nothing new. We've removed all that. You must learn to *see* differently, that shouldn't be difficult now that we've saved you from blindness. For instance, there's politics and philosophy. And the enormous cemetery that we call idealism. The brain alone won't do it, that's why we must remove the heart, I mean the lungs. Eight o'clock tomorrow morning, and no breakfast, please.

SCENE NINE

At home. Musical accompaniment.

B. O Man, give heed, what does the deep midnight say?
I slept, I slept, from a deep dream am I awakened?
The world is deep, far deeper than the day surmised.
Deep is its pain, deeper than the sorrow of the heart.
Pain says: perish, but joy desires eternity, deep deep eternity.

F. What do you mean by that?

B. The world is worse than Nietzsche surmised ... by the way, somebody said to me yesterday ... what was it? Oh yes, that Goethe and Schiller built the concentration camps...

F. You must be mad.

B. You know I have no brain, so how can I be mad? No, there may be something in it. And this morning somebody told me on the phone that SS Generals Fichte, Hegel, and Kant have been acquitted by the High Court in Frankfurt. They claimed they acted out of ignorance and invoked higher, almost divine authority.

F. That could be bad for our reputation abroad.

B. They certainly haven't done us much good. Nevertheless the acquittal was justified.

F. Why are you staring into the flower-pot like that?

B. Eichmann's seed in my living-room. In my own home.

F. Naturally you have to foul your own nest. You poor fool. They haven't cut your tongue out yet. Say something that isn't an insult to us.

B. In France old men poison the air with glorias and halleluias.

F. How awful!

B. In America they eat little yellow children alive.

F. Cannibals whichever way you look.

B. In Russia they tear out the hair of German scholars to weave nests for doves of peace.

F. Those flying rats.

B. In China every single fly is dragged into court and shot, because they won't stop flying.

F. The Chinese! What a people!

B. But they let their dragons fly around, they contaminate the air . . .

F. Now at last you're talking sense. I can smell it.

B. What you smell is English cabbage soup made with potato peelings.

F. Don't confuse me. I'm only a woman.

B. The Negroes are getting whiter every day . . .

F. Who told you that?

B. The Jews, who are building a new ark. This time they mean to go on board before it's too late.

F. Experience has taught the sly to be sly.

B. Christ is going to be excommunicated soon. It seems the Pope was the fruit of his unnatural relations with God.

F. That's a real scandal. How do you know all these things?

B. My hearing is better than ever.

F. You'd better have your ears cut off.

SCENE TEN

n the forest

. In spite of it all you still look quite intelligent.

. Was the heart operation painful?

. Not at first. It happened too fast. At the hospital they said:
your circulation. Your lungs must go. I knew what was
what as soon as the beating stopped.

. How could you know that? Your brain is gone.

. But not my ears. I've still got my ears, and they don't
hear the throbbing any more. Something is wrong. It must
be.

. It takes time. You get used to it, same as you get used to
thinking without a brain. The forest is a great teacher. Can
you still hear this?

. Yes.	*Forest music.*
. And this?	*A Mahler symphony.*
. Yes.	
. And this too?	*Mozart Requiem.*
. Yes. I hear everything.	
. How about this?	*Roaring, screaming, tumult.*

. Yes. Everything.

. You say you hear everything and you don't bat an eyelash.
You stand there silent and gaping as if you'd been whipped.
No, I don't believe it. Anybody who gives no sign is deaf.
Have your ears cut off, my good man, that may improve
your hearing.

. Have my ears cut off?

. But not now. Now it's time to work. Every single root has
to come out to make room for the new.

*Heavy breathing, digging, chopping. The men sing softly,
a melancholy Gregorian chant.*

CHORUS. Dig, dig, dig to the very last root . . .
SOLO. When everything
    is done
    and nothing flowers
    in all this land,
    when copse and tree and man
    are gone
    we bring new seeds.
CHORUS. Dig, dig, dig till nothing remains.

SCENE ELEVEN

At home. The same sounds as in Scene Nine

F. You come and go. This isn't a hotel. You find your table
   set and your bed made, but you're not at home.
B. I'm not at home anywhere, wife. Don't be cruel to me. The
   forest grows in my brain. Every pine needle a nail in my
   flesh. The mountain has buried me. Inside me there is a
   hole bigger than the ocean and the screaming of a thousand
   animals. I can't stand the voices. (*In despair.*) Help me,
   help me. The screaming never stops.
F. What kind of a forest is it where you lose your reason?
B. I lost my reason with the doctor, with you, with good helpful
   people. In the forest I lost my life. My auricles and ventricles are in the hospital. The doctor has my reason, I still
   have my ears. And recently the Boss said to me: You're
   deaf. Off with your ears.
F. What in God's name do you hear?
B (*musical accompaniment*). Listen! . . .
    the first screams,
    the mill of life,
    the breathing of the stones,

the evil eyes of a dead fish,
a hand clutches a throat
   (*Smiling and almost serene, yet sad.*)
an axe is in the earth, handle and all. A child has planted
this new tree.
Do you hear? Just listen, listen . . .
It all goes so slowly –
the snails, so slowly . . .

ℱ. You can hear all that?

ℬ (*astonished*). You really don't hear it? Which world are you living in?

ℱ (*astonished*). Which world? Are there two?

ℬ. Are there two? If there were only two! There are a thousand, a hundred thousand, aeons of worlds, worlds full of worlds, as many worlds as there are atoms. (*With conviction.*) I am in every one. (*He laughs.*) Now they're gnashing their teeth . . .

ℱ. Who?

ℬ. The atoms. (*Laughing.*) Gnashing their teeth.
   He laughs hysterically. The gnashing of teeth is heard.

ℱ. You're joking.

ℬ. It's no joke. But I like to laugh.
   They both laugh.

ℱ. But now it's time to be serious. Please have your ears cut off.

SCENE TWELVE

At the doctor's. The sound of a sawmill.

ℱ. Cut his ears off.

ᴍ. His ears?

ℱ. He hears his skin.

ᴍ. Should I cut his skin off?

F. He's always putting his fingers in his ears.

M. Should I cut his fingers off too?

F. We've got to help him, cure him. He's very sick . . .

M. Cure a sick man? What would become of us if we were to cure every sick man? The world is full of sick people . . .

F (*imploring*). Please, doctor. We've got to do something for him . . .

M. We'll see. Ears, skin, fingers. An expensive operation. But we'll see.

F. Now that his brain and heart are gone, he's hypersensitive. What shall we do?

M. Don't worry. (*Aside.*) Ears, skin, fingers. Oh well! Not easy. Hypersensitive. We'll have to put it this way . . . My dear man, just one more operation. It won't take long . . . Unfortunately, your ears will have to go. Your fingers too . . .

B. My fingers?

M. . . . And, I'm sorry to say, your skin. To forestall deafness, rheumatism and skin diseases.

B. I have confidence in medicine.

M. That's a sensible attitude. After this final amputation you can take it easy. You should feel much better.

B. Doctor?

M. Yes.

B. Doctor . . . Is it really necessary? When my ears, skin, and fingers are in your bucket, what will be left of the man? . . .

M. You can't be expected to understand such things. I'm the doctor. I'm trying to help you in the best possible way. I certainly wouldn't want to harm you.

B. You're trying to help me in the best possible way, you certainly wouldn't want to harm me . . .

M. Of course not. Your case is critical . . .

B. I am a critical case . . .

M. Critical but not unusual. Nowadays we have many patients with your complaints . . .

B. Really, doctor?

1. Definitely. The result of the atomic explosion. Nuclear fission has already begun. It's not in the air that we see the consequences, but in the human brain.

3. Why not abandon nuclear fission, doctor?

A. That is impossible. But it's perfectly possible to eliminate man with scalpel and saw ... In your own interest.

3. In that case I'll be here at eight o'clock tomorrow morning on an empty stomach. No breakfast.

A. That's very wise of you.

SCENE THIRTEEN

In the forest. Trees are being felled and men are singing as in earlier scenes. Groaning.

3. Who's groaning? It's not me. What does it mean? Something must be done. Surgery and medicine to forestall the worst. Brain removed, heart removed, air let out of my lungs, skin peeled off my body, eyes gouged out, fingers sawed, and now my ears cut off to enable me to speak. They've forgotten my tongue ... Bla-bla-bla-bla-bla. (*Louder and louder.*) Bla-bla-bla-bla.

A. Quiet! What is this blubbering? What's got into you?

B. Bla-bla-bla-bla-bla. The Devil has eaten me hollow ...

A. Stop that bleating. They've left you your tongue. What more do you want?

B. Bla-bla-bla-bla. Rip my tongue out.

A (*in a tone of grave admonishment*). Not your tongue. Your tongue? No. Don't have your tongue removed.

B. Rip my tongue out. Bla, bla, bla ... it's still moving, bla, bla, bla, bla ...

A. You ought to be glad. If you didn't have your tongue, how would we know how you're getting along? No, your tongue must stay. The rest isn't so important. The main thing is the tongue ... listen to my men singing. (*Gregorian chan* *of the men at work.*) ... Listen to that ... merrily the worl goes on, as our great poet ...

B (*screams, whimpers*). Out with my tongue! Please cut my tongue out. I don't want to scream ...

A. Animals scream too or speak or wail. Animals are always crying, but in a self-respecting way. Your whimpering is disgusting. (*He cries out.*) Animals, speak!

First softly then louder and louder a barking, howling, cackling, piping, chirping, roaring and growling which merge into forest music.

Self-respect. Man needs self-respect. Have this tongue removed? Ridiculous. Don't articulate so much, then your meaning will be clear.

SCENE FOURTEEN

At home. Wild music.

K 1. Yeah, yeah ...

K 2. Tch-tch-tch ...

The resounding laughter of many people.

B. Moo ...

K 1. Ts ts ts ts ...   *Laughter.*

B. Brrr-ooooh.

K 1. Ffff ... sh-sh-sh ...

K 2 (*singing*). Bow-wow-wow.   *Laughter*

B. Brrrr.   *Brief barking.*

F. Now I don't understand you at all any more ...

B (*speaks almost unintelligibly*). My tongue. Take my tongue away. My tongue.

Loud: voices, beat music, pop songs, all incomprehensible. *B howls like a wolf.*

SCENE FIFTEEN

At the doctor's. The sound of a metronome.

M. After our last conversation, my good man, one last remark. Your wife has asked me to do something about your tongue. On this point, I cannot agree. Not that a tongue extraction could do any harm in your case, but there are practical considerations. First the question of my fee . . .

B. Yes . . .

M. Up until now you have benefited by every conceivable kind of insurance. Social, personal, human, special and private. The Association paid.

B. Yes . . .

M. Thus far the Bird Impersonators' Association has paid for everything, except what it didn't pay for. Your fingers and skin, for instance. I paid for them out of my own pocket.

B. Yes.

M. For humane reasons.

B. Yes.

M. Medicine is almost a philanthropic enterprise, but not quite. The Bird Impersonators' Association has been extremely generous. But even generosity has its limits. As a bird impersonator, you are, if you'll pardon the expression, *hors de combat* for the present. We understand physical defects perfectly. Mental derangement is more complex . . .

B. Yes . . .

M (*reads aloud*). . . . the member undertakes, see Statutes 15-B, to notify the president or his representative immediately of the following:

    (*a*) Death;

    (*b*) Loss of voice;

    (*c*) Financial bankruptcy;

    (*d*) Inability to participate in weekly exercises.

B. Yes.

M. To date you have reported nothing, absolutely nothing, to the Association . . . Right?

B. Yes.

M. I continue – (*He reads*): In case of failure to observe the rules and regulations, see Statutes, Part I, the Association is (*With emphasis.*) under no circumstances liable for expenses incurred by a member in consequence of illness (including mental). In short, such expenses are your own obligation.

B. Yes.

M. Of course you are not to blame, but the obligation remains yours . . . A debt is a debt and I cannot be expected to pay yours. Right?

B. Yes.

M. Kindly tender my compliments and respects to your wife. I wish you the best of luck.

B. Yes.

M. Good-bye.

B (*stands up and leaves*). Yes.

M (*calling after him*). You have been careless, extremely careless.

B (*roars*). Yes!

SCENE SIXTEEN

At home. The ticking of a clock. A cuckoo clock. The cuckoo calls three times.

F. What are you mulling over?

B. My guilt. I've been extremely careless.

F. What are you staring for?

B. The old days. Now I see it for the first time. The days before I sang with the birds in the woods, before fear caught up with me, when I still had a skin to peel, when I still had voices for my ears, things to grasp, thoughts in my head, work in the forest, fear of eternity. Fear. What's become of my fear? Now I'm sitting with you in the kitchen. The tea tastes like dust, the bread tastes like wood, and the children have grown up. What now?

F. Look into the future, the doctor says, to see what's coming. Now that the future is invisible, see the future. Open your eyes. Now that your eyes hardly open, open your eyes.

B. Open my eyes. Yes.

F. Open your eyes . . . for God's sake.

B. They won't open.

F. Look. The light is hanging over the table.

B. And who's hanging over there across the street?

F. Oh him! That's a crazy man, he hanged himself three days ago. Better look at the new linoleum, how beautifully it covers the floor.

B. Is that a cat or a child lying in the gutter and screaming?

F. Oh, that's one of the neighbours' children. They put him out in the street so he wouldn't be in the way at home. Better look at the broken chair in your own kitchen, and the walls that ought to be whitewashed.

B. What is that twisted frame down there between the cars?

F. People who escape from the woods every day. Simple people.

B. It sounds simple. I see it differently. (*He opens the window and calls out into the street.*) Stop, people. Stop! Don't go on. Turn back.

F (*closes the window*). Close the window. What will the neighbours think of us?

B (*opens the window violently*). Neighbours, what do you think of us?

Whistling and laughing in the street.

F. They're laughing at us. (*She closes the window.*) Stop that
We need something to cheer us up. Let's see what there is
on TV.

*She turns a knob. Sounds of television. She keeps turning
the knob. Quickly changing sounds: football game, music-hall
play, etc.*

Now where are you going? You can't see anything.

She turns off the television. The voices stop abruptly.

B. I'll find him.

F. Watch out for the cars.

B. Don't worry. It's only a short walk. I'm going to give it one
last try

F. Do you more good to rest. Stay at home.

Forest music.

The doctor has done so much for you. You mustn't molest
him.

B. Only this last try. I've got a suggestion he can't turn down

The door closes.

F. That's something I've got to see. No really, I've got to see
it.

The door closes again.

SCENE SEVENTEEN

At the doctor's.

M. Kindly open your mouth. (B *bellows like a bull.*) Fine. Now
say Aaaah. (B *roars like a lion.*) Excellent. Now please remove
your shirt – that's it. (*Sounds of railway trains and loco-
motives, suddenly breaking off.*) Just want to examine your
chest. Thank you. Splendid. Seems to be in good shape.
Now cross your legs, you're going to feel a slight blow, this
leg a little higher, I'm going to strike it with this rubber

hammer. It won't hurt. (*A slight tapping, followed by the sound of breaking china.*) And now, let's see your throat. Excellent. The forest air was the right thing, did your larynx good. Now kindly rest your head there – a little lower, that's better. The knife you see up there is a kind of axe, named after my celebrated colleague Guillot. It's going to fall when I press the button – but it won't inconvenience you and definitely will not hurt.

We hear the falling of the guillotine and a short scream. The woman utters a second short scream.

There we are, Madam, your husband is entirely cured. Do you wish to take him home, or should we keep him here?

F *bursts into sobs. Music as at the beginning, but more monotonous. Short, suddenly dying phrases*

F. How much do I owe you?

M. You don't owe me a penny. He paid for it all in advance. We've been experimenting with the guillotine lately for hay fever and countless other disorders. And now we know that there's nothing better for birdman's melancholia.

F. You've done so much for my husband.

M. On the contrary, science owes him a debt of gratitude.

The metronome ticks.